T0323579

Cambridge Elements ☰

Elements in Critical Issues in Teacher Education
edited by
Tony Loughland
University of New South Wales
Andy Gao
University of New South Wales
Hoa T. M. Nguyen
University of New South Wales

WHO AM I AS A TEACHER?

Migrant Teachers' Redefined Professional Identity

Annika Käck
Stockholm University

CAMBRIDGE
UNIVERSITY PRESS

Shaftesbury Road, Cambridge CB2 8EA, United Kingdom

One Liberty Plaza, 20th Floor, New York, NY 10006, USA

477 Williamstown Road, Port Melbourne, VIC 3207, Australia

314–321, 3rd Floor, Plot 3, Splendor Forum, Jasola District Centre, New Delhi – 110025, India

103 Penang Road, #05–06/07, Visioncrest Commercial, Singapore 238467

Cambridge University Press is part of Cambridge University Press & Assessment, a department of the University of Cambridge.

We share the University's mission to contribute to society through the pursuit of education, learning and research at the highest international levels of excellence.

www.cambridge.org
Information on this title: www.cambridge.org/9781009494472

DOI: 10.1017/9781009341042

© Annika Käck 2024

When citing this work, please include a reference to the DOI 10.1017/9781009341042

First published 2024

A catalogue record for this publication is available from the British Library.

ISBN 978-1-009-49447-2 Hardback
ISBN 978-1-009-34101-1 Paperback
ISSN 2755-1202 (online)
ISSN 2755-1199 (print)

Who Am I as a Teacher?

Migrant Teachers' Redefined Professional Identity

Elements in Critical Issues in Teacher Education

DOI: 10.1017/9781009341042
First published online: November 2024

Annika Käck
Stockholm University

Author for correspondence: Annika Käck, annika.kack@specped.su.se

Abstract: Redefined transformative learning refers to learning that implies a change in the learner's identity, which includes cognitive, emotional, and social dimensions and is something all teachers, in this case migrant teachers, experience and negotiate when meeting a new educational context. 'Who am I as a teacher in a new country?' migrant teachers ask themselves. To understand oneself as a teacher, one must identify and coordinate the past and present with a future direction, which causes migrant teachers to talk about a transformed professional identity with additional skills. This Element concerns migrant teachers' transformation, how they redefine their professional identity, and how to support this in teacher education.

This Element also has a video abstract: www.cambridge.org/EITE_Kack

Keywords: teacher education, migrant teachers, redefined identity, transformative learning

ISBNs: 9781009494472 (HB), 9781009341011 (PB), 9781009341042 (OC)
ISSNs: 2755-1202 (online), 2755-1199 (print)

Contents

1 Introduction   3

2 Migrant Teachers and Transformative Learning   16

3 Teacher Educators from Other Countries   48

4 Conclusion and Future Directions   58

   References   65

Preface

In an era where global mobility and cultural intersections increase, the experiences of migrant teachers in the Swedish educational system emerge as a narrative of redefined transformative learning experiences. This text explores the challenges and successes these educators encounter as they enter a wide range of familiar and unfamiliar educational environments. The Element aims to shine a light on their experiences, illustrating the struggles and the profound opportunities for growth and learning that arise from such a transition. This goes both ways; Swedish teacher education and Swedish teachers have a lot to learn from these competent colleagues worldwide. The text also contemplates the future of migrant-centred education in Sweden, considering the potential changes and developments that could further support and enhance the integration and contribution of migrant teachers and Swedish teacher education.

Through a blend of theoretical insights and empirical research, this text paints a picture of the migrant teachers' experiences. At the heart of this exploration is redefined transformative learning, a transformative journey not just about acquiring new teaching methods; it is a more profound, more introspective reshaping of their teacher identities. It is important to say that all teachers are on this journey as well; however, in this Element, we will look into the specific experiences migrant teachers express. More than a mere acquisition of new teaching techniques, this journey represents a profound internal shift—a re-evaluation and re-definition of their professional selves. It also highlights how migrant teachers enrich the educational landscape with their perspectives and experiences, contributing to a more diverse, inclusive learning environment.

In this Element, migrant teachers' voices will be heard, which has always been important to me as a teacher educator and researcher. In this perspective, we can move from 'otherness' to 'togetherness' since we have much to learn from each other, thus developing education at different levels. I have been involved in education and development for more than 30 years, with a background as an upper secondary teacher and in special education, which reflects my research, which primarily focuses on teachers' competencies and teacher education. Today, I am director of studies at the Department of Special Education, teach in teacher education and am involved at the Centre for the Advancement of University Teaching, Stockholm University.

Writing this Element has been joyful, as migrant teachers are an important group to me; they have been part of my work for many years, and I meet them every semester, either as a teacher responsible for courses in special education or while conducting research. Further, my colleagues Katie Obeid and Manal Musa write about themselves (see Sections 3.1 and 3.2), giving insights into the transition as teachers from other countries. Larissa Mickwitz and I conducted research interviews together, and I have always appreciated working with her. I valued the interesting editorial discussions with Linnea Hössjer and am thankful to Susanna Malm, and Tove Linné, National Coordinators of the bridging programme, for reading and fact-checking Section 1. I am most grateful to Hoa Nguyen, the main editor of this Element, for her invaluable advice and encouragement during the writing process, to editor Tony Loughland, who contacted me initially, and to editor Andy Gao. Lastly, thanks to all the excellent refugee and migrant teachers I have met as an educator. I want to end with a quotation from my sister, a principal who has worked with education for over 25 years: 'One of the best teachers I ever hired was from Syria. She managed everything.'

Plan of the Element

This Element is based on my research and experiences as a teacher educator and researcher, working with migrant teachers from approximately 100 countries over many years. The intention is to discuss professional identity transformation and the unfamiliar ways of thinking and practising migrant teachers' experiences in a new educational context. Section 1, 'Introduction', introduces migrant teachers in Swedish teacher education, what the Migrant World Values Survey tells us about migrated people in Sweden and the fundamental values and tasks that the Swedish curricula are based on. This forms a background to why migrated teachers redefine their professional identity, which will be further explored in the following sections. Section 2, 'Migrant Teachers and Transformative Learning', describes the theoretical foundations I often use in my research projects and teaching designs. Illeris, professor emeritus in lifelong learning, defines transformative learning as 'learning which implies a change in the learner's identity' (2014a, 2014b p. 40, 2014c), including three dimensions of learning: cognitive, emotional, and social. I will then reflect on the findings from my previous studies on migrant teachers within the context of Swedish teacher education. Finally, I present the results of my current research project. Section 3, 'Teacher Educators From Other Countries', will go more in-depth about two teacher educators, colleagues of mine at Stockholm University, who have a background as teachers in two different countries in the Middle East. They write about their transition into a new educational context. I will summarise and reflect on their stories in relation to redefined transformative learning and identity. In Section 4, 'Conclusion And Future Directions', some conclusions will be drawn and summarised based on the former sections. We will look into "Migrant-Centred Teacher Education" and "Future Directions".

1 Introduction

This section will initially unravel the complexities of Sweden's education system and the experiences of migrant teachers within it, providing an in-depth look at the government's support in bridging the professional qualifications of immigrants. The narrative gives insight into these integration efforts and the Swedish bridging programmes which support migrant teachers' transfer into the Swedish educational system. Since the Swedish curricula are based on fundamental Swedish values with pedagogical implications, gaining insight into the Migrant World Values Survey can be particularly enlightening. Lastly, to understand migrant teachers' development and transformation, we dig into literature concerning teachers' beliefs and professional identity as they are the foundation of being a teacher.

1.1 Migrant Teachers in Swedish Teacher Education

The Swedish government acknowledges and values immigrants' professional qualifications, foreign overseas academic education, and experiences. Thus, the Swedish government allocates resources to programmes that supplement immigrants' education with specific requirements for working in Sweden. The programmes are designed for nurses, dentists, physicians, physiotherapists, psychologists, biomedical analysts, social workers, engineers, lawyers, architects, teachers, and other professionals. This Element explores the professional identities of migrant teachers and their educational needs in relation to teacher training. It is imperative to note that a Swedish teacher studying a bridging, supplementary programme in another country requires the same kind of support this programme offers.

There are bridging programmes in other countries to meet the specific qualifications in each country (Collins & Reid, 2012; Cruickshank, 2022; Marom, 2017; Proyer et al., 2019). For a more comprehensive understanding of the situation in Germany, Austria, and Sweden, please refer to the R/EQUAL project website, focusing on the requalification of newly immigrated and refugee teachers in Europe (www.hf.uni-koeln.de/immigrated-and-refugee-teachers-requal/). I collaborated with teacher educators in this two-year project and met refugee and immigrant teachers in Sweden, Germany, and Austria, recognising their shared experiences. Our project aimed to enhance knowledge and provide guidance to other higher education institutions that want to create bridging programmes. Those included a theoretical framework with a comparative analysis of the current situation of (recently) immigrated and refugee teachers (spring 2019), a manual for language learning in a translingual learning setting, a toolbox of educational methods for working on the topic of heterogeneity and school considering the European anti-discrimination policy, a digital library with references to scientific papers and studies on teacher education and (re-)professionalisation, an evaluation report regarding the participatory approach chosen in R/EQUAL, a general guideline including all results as well as further recommendations to set up a programme for (recently) immigrated and refugee teachers.

Teachers with a foreign degree are usually trained in their countries with the expectation of teaching in that specific country, not to be teachers in other countries or international teachers. Terms such as internationally trained teachers and overseas-trained teachers are sometimes used in studies (Marom, 2019; Miller, 2018; Proyer et al., 2019); however, they may imply that the teachers' education was aimed towards international work, which is not the case. Additionally, terms that can be used to describe the participants are migrant teachers, teachers with a foreign teaching degree, teachers with a migration background, or immigrant teachers. The issue with this terminology is that it labels teachers with foreign teaching degrees as migrants. How long is one categorised as a migrant, and does this risk 'othering'? However, these terms have been used in research (Bense, 2016; Collins & Reid, 2012; Donlevy, Mejerkord, & Rajania, 2016; Ennser-Kananen & Ruohotie-Lyhty, 2023; Käck, 2019; Peeler, 2015; Walsh et al., 2011) and dissertations (Asmus, 2015; Edwards, 2014). They are also used in the project R/EQUAL, the Requalification of (recently) immigrated and refugee teachers in Europe in addition to internationally trained teachers (Proyer et al., 2019). There are plenty of reasons migrant teachers come to Sweden, for example, marriage, work, education, family, refugee status, etc. The common denominator is that they are teachers with a background in migration. Therefore, the term 'refugee' is not universally appropriate, as not all migrants in Sweden have a history of forced migration. The word migrant teacher is used in this Element without setting a frame for how long one has been a migrant. It means that one has a teaching degree from another country and has migrated to Sweden.

In order to define how countries should organise educational systems, European countries, such as the Nordic ones, use specific international guidelines. One example is the Professional Qualifications Directive, which helps countries to recognise professional qualifications and foreign education (Council of Europe, 1997, 2010; Nordic Council of Ministers, 2017; Malm, 2019). The Swedish government aims to integrate qualified teachers into teacher education programmes. This aligns the teachers' competencies with specific Swedish requirements (Ministry of Education and Research in Sweden, 2011, 2014b, 2016). Certification is required for permanent employment as a teacher in Sweden since teaching is regulated. The Swedish National Agency for Education authorises and issues a diploma of certification.

The government initiative 'Further Education for Foreign Teachers (the label changed nationally in 2023 to Bridging Programme for Teachers Educated Abroad)' [Utländska Lärares Vidareutbildning, now nationally changed to Utlandsutbildade lärares vidareutbildning] allows teachers with foreign teaching degrees to study at six Swedish universities. The universities offering supplementary education for teachers with foreign teaching degrees include Stockholm University, University of Gothenburg, Linköping University, Malmö University, Umeå University, and Örebro University. The Swedish Council for Higher Education is responsible for evaluating this programme. This initiative, a bridging supplementary programme that began in 2007 as a government mandate, offers supplementary education for teachers with a migration background who want to be qualified to teach in Swedish schools. The initiative has two central aims: to provide migrant teachers with more opportunities for employment in Swedish schools and to utilise their competence. The population consists of individuals from over 100 countries with university teaching degrees (Malm, 2019).

Table 1 showcases the number of teachers and applicants admitted to the supplementary programme in all six universities, reported to the Ministry of Education and Research in Sweden by the National Coordinator at Stockholm University (Cornelius & Bredänge, 2011; Malm, 2022; Malm & Åström, 2019; Stockholm University, 2017). Between 2008 and 2022, 5946 migrant teachers were admitted to the bridging programme for teachers.

There is a collaboration between The Swedish National Agency for Education and the Swedish Council for Higher Education to assess foreign education. When foreign and Swedish teacher education gaps arise, Swedish teacher education programmes offer supplementary education. In 2007, a national steering group was established, comprising representatives from all six universities, which included participants from all six universities: Stockholm University, University of Gothenburg, Linköping University, Malmö University, Umeå University, and Örebro University, with Stockholm University as the coordinator. It ensures the quality of education. Moreover, the collaboration extends to teacher unions, the Swedish National Agency for Education and the Swedish Council for Higher Education.

To be eligible for the programme, migrant teachers must have an upper secondary school skill level in Swedish. Additionally, they must have a teaching diploma from a country outside Sweden (Cornelius & Bredänge, 2011). Even though teachers with migrant backgrounds have different teaching experiences and education lengths, they all become student teachers while attending the bridging programme. This is because they study within ordinary teacher education programmes; thus, they simultaneously train in professional

Table 1 The number of applicants and admitted
teachers to the bridging programme

Year	Applicants	Admitted
2008	285	202
2009	574	347
2010	480	304
2011	607	320
2012	543	358
2013	510	366
2014	643	433
2015	770	438
2016	922	494
2017	828	461
2018	1010	577
2019	1284	498
2020	1613	495
2021	1331	322
2022	1044	331
In sum	**12444**	5946

development and pre-service. When teachers with migrant backgrounds attend the education programme, an individualised supplementary study plan is created. The plan consists of up to 120 ECTS (European Credit Transfer and Accumulation System) credits, encompassing higher education courses. It includes educational science for teaching professions, subject studies and subject didactics, and study school, which provides a didactic and pedagogical environment.

Both study planning and study guidance are individual and follow the migrant teachers through the entire educational programme. One reason for a longer study time is the discrepancy in the workplace between the former country and Sweden. For example, even though a person has been a teacher in mathematics from grades 1 to 9 in his/her country, there are no such teaching jobs in a Swedish school. If one is a mathematics teacher in Sweden, one also has additional subjects. The teachers adhere to their study plans and enrol in existing courses within the standard teacher education programmes. Additionally, they study a course called 'To be a Teacher in Sweden' [Att bli lärare i Sverige], worth 22.5 ECTS credits. This introductory course is designed for the governmental initiative and aims to improve Swedish language skills, orally and in academic writing. Moreover, the migrant teachers study different aspects of the Swedish educational system, including national regulations and requirements, values, and the grading system.

Lastly, a placement period takes place where they put theoretical knowledge to practical use in Swedish schools.

The Swedish effort to integrate migrant teachers into its educational system through bridging programmes aligns with findings from the Migrant World Values Survey (MWVS) in Sweden. The MWVS revealed how migrants perceive integration and their values in relation to their new society. It is a topic that migrant teachers wish to discuss in relation to their professional identity during supplementary education (Käck et al., 2018a). Understanding these perceptions is crucial to effective curriculum planning and addressing teachers' multifaceted professional identities in a culturally diverse environment.

1.2 Migrant World Values Survey (MWVS) in Sweden

World Values Survey is an organisation that, since 1981, has measured values and social norms worldwide (www.worldvaluessurvey.org). They have conducted surveys in approximately 100 countries, allowing researchers and authorities worldwide to use this empirical data. The so-called seventh wave of the survey is going on right now. The survey comprises 290 questions, gauging cultural values, attitudes, and beliefs across various domains, including family, child-rearing, religion, gender, equality, education, health, safety, social tolerance, trust, and views on multilateral institutions.

In summary, the survey reflects how people in different cultures think about values and social norms shared in society. The seventh wave introduces new topics such as justice, moral principles, corruption, and accountability. A world cultural map is generated, consolidating the values into a single coordinate for each country, as depicted in The Inglehart-Welzel World Cultural Map – World Values Survey 7, 2022 (see Figure 1). According to the World Values Survey, Sweden and other Nordic countries rank highest globally in secular and individualistic values. Conversely, the cultural map also illustrates societies with more religious, traditional values and hierarchical structures.

Answers from migrants have been absent; however, this has been solved in a Migrant World Values Survey (MWVS) conducted in Sweden in 2018 within 54 municipalities (Puranen, 2019). The MWVS conducted a survey which focused on non-European migrants who lived in Sweden, intending to know more about how this respondent group viewed themselves and their new home country. Bi Puranen led the research project, drawing on her roles at the Institute for Future Studies, which provided the study's framework, and as Secretary General of the World Values Survey. The Swedish Ministry of Employment, government offices, and the counties of Värmland and Skåne supported the project. A total of 6,516 migrants, representing 130 countries, completed the

The Inglehart-Welzel World Cultural Map 2023

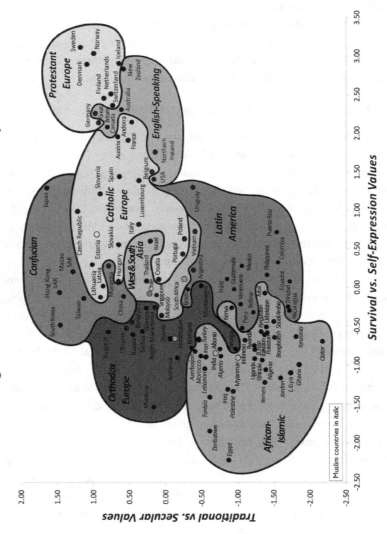

Figure 1 The Inglehart-Welzel World Cultural Map – World Values Survey 7 (2023).

Source: www.worldvaluessurvey.org/.

survey, available in languages including Swedish, English, Arabic, Dari, Somali, Tigrinya, and Turkish, ensuring a representative sample of immigrants in Sweden. Migrants in Sweden are a heterogeneous group regarding cultural and educational backgrounds. The survey, mirroring the seventh World Values Survey (WVS), consisted of the same 200 questions, supplemented by additional ones. These extra questions were aimed at understanding how values and norms might shift when individuals move from one country to another. Additionally, 200 respondents participated in semi-structured interviews, and 44 did in-depth interviews. Finally, the results compared answers from the origin country and Sweden. The results and analysis are compiled in the book 'Med migranternas röst. Den subjektiva integrationen.' [With the Voice of Migrants. The Subjective Integration.] (Puranen, 2019).

The MWVS study aimed to learn more about how non-European migrants in Sweden view integration and their values and norms. Even though migrants expressed that they have better opportunities to obtain an education in Sweden, expectations for work were harder to fulfil. While a majority of respondents endorsed gender equality, they perceived it as overly pronounced in Sweden. The results visualised in the WVS cultural map show substantial differences in emancipative values between migrants from Iraq, Iran, and Turkey and people in their country of origin, showing that these values change to a large extent when moving to Sweden. According to Puranen (2019), 75 per cent of the migrants originated from authoritarian states. Values vary in different cultures, often regarding living conditions.

Reflecting on the MWVS is crucial because the Swedish curriculum, rooted in fundamental values, significantly influences teachers' professional identity and responsibilities. The MWVS findings underscore the need for Sweden's education system, intrinsically value-based and characterised by democratic ideals, to consider these multicultural perspectives and experiences. Particularly for migrant teachers, whose personal and work identities may transform due to cultural shifts, the implications of these diverse values become pivotal. Navigating this intersection of migrant values and Swedish norms is integral to teaching and learning in today's Sweden. However, it is valuable for Swedish teacher educators to become aware that Sweden, which can appear extreme to others, is situated in the right corner of the World Surveys cultural 2015–2022 map.

1.3 The Swedish Curriculum

As we can see in Section 1.2, Sweden is a secular, non-hierarchical, and individualistic country in the World Values Survey. In addition, the Swedish school system and teacher education are value-based. Why is this important in this Element? This is crucial because virtually all migrant teachers wish to discuss these topics and frequently bring them up during seminars, their placement period, and focus group interviews. All national curricula underscore fundamental democratic values, as strongly emphasised by the Swedish government and parliament. The laws, curricula, and ordinances determine the value base in Sweden (The National Agency for Education, 2013, 2019, 2022; Ministry of Education and Research, 2011, 2014a). The initial section of all national curricula, spanning roughly 20 pages, is titled 'The Fundamental Values and Tasks of the School: Overall Goals and Guidelines'. Every teacher must support students' uniqueness, gender, sexual orientation, ethnic affiliation, solidarity between people and values, belief systems, and personal standpoints (religious and non-religious). It is stated that the teacher should take each student's needs, circumstances, experiences, and thinking as the starting point and that students must take personal responsibility for their studies and working environment. The last sentence has pedagogical implications on how to work as a teacher. This is an example of a statement that affects teachers' beliefs and practices since it has implications for pedagogy in the Swedish context. For instance, teachers must consider each student's needs, experiences, and thought processes when planning and conducting lessons. Another is fostering social learning by using groups and letting their reflections and experiences be at the centre. Thus, there are implications for teacher educators since university education must support students' making critical assessments, working with social learning, being independent, and taking responsibility for their learning (Ministry of Education and Research, 1992, 2014a). As can be seen, pedagogical work is influenced both by mandatory school and teacher education. Moreover, digital competence is of great importance in the curriculum. These principles affect migrant teachers' practices and professional belief systems, thus their identity as teachers. It is of great importance to distinguish between an individual's identity and beliefs and the teacher's professional identity. As an individual, one may think and believe whatever one wants, protected by the Constitution. However, as professionals, teachers are required to uphold the school's fundamental values. What is written as fundamental values and beliefs in the curricula also impacts and directs how to act and teach as a teacher. However, this is not per se evident in Sweden or other countries. One migrant teacher told me, during a seminar, that she came from a democratic country and taught about democracy but realised that she did not teach democratically. Further, the former country's values can be a motivating element to continue to teach. Kwee (2023) revealed that traditional Confucian values, supportive learning environments, and goal attainment motivated Chinese teachers to continue teaching in Australia. Blending the old and new can support a new teacher identity with additional skills in a new country without losing the former ones (Käck, 2019). Swedish curricula, steeped in democratic values, directly shape teaching practices, impacting educators' professional identities, including those of migrant teachers. As we pivot to teachers' beliefs and professional identity, it is essential to remember that Sweden's pedagogical context, including digital competence, provides a backdrop for teacher development and identity formation.

1.4 Teachers' Beliefs and Professional Identity

A teacher's belief system consists of a holistic view of learning and how the school content relates to society. This affects the teaching and learning environment, shapes learning practices, and influences the way they interact with students and how they view their role as teachers. Beliefs about teaching and learning, integral to teachers' professional identity, involve interpreting and reinterpreting experiences. These are context-dependent and variable over time (Dos Santos, 2022; Guskey, 2002; Kalaja et al., 2016; Korthagen, 2013; Lee & Schallert, 2016; Stensmo, 1994, 2007). Beliefs about teaching and learning are a system. This belief system is at the core of the teacher's professional identity. Yip et al.'s (2022) findings reveal that migrant teachers' professional identity is critical in the professional transition, linking it to employment status, beliefs, and attitudes towards teaching. Further, Yip (2023) identified professional vulnerability as a critical emotion affecting the teachers' professional transition and identified a shift in migrant teachers' professional identity with a shift in their beliefs and skills as part of their new educational context. Furthermore, Bressler and Rotter (2017) link migrant teachers' professional identity with the expectations of policymakers and colleagues. Therefore, cultural, social, and political contexts are significant factors in identity formation. They advocate for more support for migrant teachers' reflections on their biography and expectations from others (due to their migrant background) and what this implies for their professional identity. Three types of professional identities were identified among migrant teachers. The first considers their life experience as migrants of utmost importance; the second rejects the relevance of their migrant background, emphasising their pedagogical competence instead. The third type falls somewhere between these two. Migrant teachers could experience othering by their colleagues and culturalisation of students' difficulties, concerns that must be addressed in teacher education (Bressler & Rotter, 2017). Further, the problems of getting their credits validated and navigating the organizational structures could be an additional challenge (Ennerberg & Economou, 2022).

Miller (2018) has found clear evidence that even though migrant teachers are important contributors to the workforce, they are merely surviving and coping with the new educational system. However, less evidence has been found that they are thriving or flourishing, aspects that necessitate government observation. This is evident when teachers' vulnerabilities are taken into consideration. Yips (2023) identified that professional vulnerability affected the migrant teachers' transition, impacted by their perceived teaching competence by students, parents, and colleagues. When valued, it strengthens their self-confidence. However, sometimes, these migrant teachers felt that principals or colleagues did not trust their teaching competence, additionally questioned by parents, with increasing vulnerability as a result. This professional vulnerability persisted for a long time when migrant teachers were confronted with situations related to their teaching competence, bad-mannered students, and social isolation in the workplace. Yip (2023) recognised that the lack of a network contributed to the teachers' vulnerability.

Kwee (2020) identified various challenges faced by migrated teachers in Australia. They were getting their qualifications accredited, discrepancies in classroom management, and experiences of racism and discrimination. In order to aid their integration, there is a need for a support system to help them in their career choices. Despite access to bridging programmes and courses on local curricula, classroom dynamics, and Australian children's language, migrant teachers were often urged to adopt an Australian teaching style, a pressure that contributed to dissatisfaction and disillusionment with some bridging programmes (Kwee, 2020). Thus, teacher educators can support migrant teachers' competencies, bringing them up during seminars and letting them explore their former knowledge with the new ones together with teachers in the new country. Miller (2019) mentions social identity theory, in which the sense of who they are is based on group membership and provides a sense of belonging. Thus, the individual adopts the group's identity, conforming to their norms. The findings show that migrant teachers felt they were not taken seriously and lacked opportunities and support. They also experienced problems getting opportunities to lead, even if they desired this progression. Consequently, their roles were often confined to behaviour management and classroom teaching (Miller, 2019). However, Dos Santos (2022) argues that, despite facing challenges and culture shock as English teachers in South Korea, the international experience enhanced their teaching skills and sense of internationalisation.

All teachers, not only migrant teachers, go through continuous development throughout their professional lives. Thus, trained teachers are challenged to reconstruct, question, and interlink their beliefs and experiences with unfamiliar ones, such as the Swedish educational context. Migrant teachers in different countries need to understand what they experience as unfamiliar and why.

This helps them redefine their professional identity and teach in a new educational context (Käck et al., 2018a). When migrant teachers express their thoughts about ways of thinking and practising, teaching and learning, and how learning occurs, their teachers' beliefs form their answers.

According to Guskey (2002), teachers' beliefs and practices are essential for professional development. A consequential change in their beliefs and attitudes can occur when teachers can see evidence of increased student learning. However, Bautista and Ortega-Ruiz (2015) argue that substantial professional development is often ineffective and serves limited outcomes. Moreover, high-quality professional development is not solely event-based. It requires a long process with many elements of active learning, feedback, and follow-up support. Furthermore, teachers develop their own personal, interpretive framework during their work and education that significantly affects their teaching practice, which develops through interaction. It also influences their perception of teacher roles and their views as teachers (Kelchtermans, 2009). In order to interact, language is of utmost importance since speaking is a way to be accepted in society and their profession (Lefever et al., 2014).

This lens continues to develop throughout purposeful interaction. All teachers constantly experience professional development related to practice changes and teaching beliefs. However, Vandeyar et al. (2014) discovered that certain migrant teachers held on to former ways of knowing, believing these were superior education methods. Others struggled with what was considered a new educational paradigm, claiming that they had to make a substantial shift regarding education in the new society since their former way of teaching did not prove effective. This resulted in a negative impact on their professional identity.

Teachers' self-images are shaped by the interplay of immediate and broader education, such as policies in Iran, changing their identities. It shows that these educators face challenges reconciling personal beliefs with external demands. The findings underscore the importance of continuous professional development in relation to more comprehensive political environments (Eslamdoost, King, & Tajeddin, 2020). One potential method for facilitating this delicate transition could involve the use of a mentor. The importance of having a mentor is described by Yan (2021) as a unique experience since it links migrant teachers' personal lives with professional identities within their context and, in the end, affects their professional development. Miller (2019) also stresses the importance of a knowledgeable mentor who understands their passion for progression and the barriers they meet. Thus, a mentor could help in relation to what Lee and Schallert (2016) write about, which is how teachers must identify their past, present, and future to understand teaching and their selves. For all teachers, professional development is solely made by reconstructing and questioning their identities, which they need support to do (Bressler & Rotter, 2017). A reflective framework for professional development involves competencies, behaviour, the environment, identity, beliefs, and mission (Korthagen, 2013).

According to the literature, teachers' beliefs and confidence are related to teachers' integration of digital competence (Lawless & Pellegrino, 2007; Sadaf & Johnson, 2017), which is seen as the final frontier regarding the integration of digital technology (Ertmer, 2005). According to Cruishank (2022) and Käck (2019a), digital competence development was sought by migrant teachers. However, what kind of digital competence do teachers need, and how can they achieve this? In their literature review, Masoumi and Noroozi (2023) shed light on pivotal elements shaping the digital competence of early-career teachers. They underscore the significance of personal exploration, developmental opportunities, mentoring, and the relationship between digital proficiency and teachers' professional identities, all of which profoundly influence their pedagogical methods. In a similar vein, Skantz-Åberg et al. (2022) outline essential elements of teachers' digital competence, ranging from technological acumen to professional collaboration, emphasising its criticality in today's digitised societies.

Digital competence is essential in Swedish teacher education and schools and impacts teachers' professional identity and confidence to incorporate it into their teaching practices (Käck, 2019a). Thus, knowledge about digital technologies is helpful for teachers regarding intercultural relationships, classroom practices, and online collaboration (Chamberlin-Quinlisk, 2013). In online learning, for instance, cultural differences can affect students' engagement and satisfaction with the technological, pedagogical, and organisational components. Therefore, creating a culturally inclusive environment is of great importance (Hannon & D'Netto, 2007). Wen et al. (2023) findings highlight that those Western foreign teachers teaching at a Sino-English University in China confronted challenges on two distinct dimensions: one about cultural disparities in pedagogical practices and the other instigated by a transition towards online teaching.

Nonetheless, they gained enhanced knowledge in transnational education by utilising critical reflection as a methodological tool. Additionally, Byram (1997) states that intercultural competence consists of self-critical cultural awareness, knowledge of others, and skills to interact, relate, interpret, and value others' belief systems and behaviours. Hence, Thomas (1997) writes that a culturally sensitive pedagogy can be created and developed when cultural factors are investigated and identified. Therefore, learning and growing in a diverse cultural context should be planned, examined, and supported (Bennett, 2012; Käck et al., 2014).

1.5 Summary

Sweden wants to integrate migrant teachers by acknowledging their overseas qualifications and offering them bridging programmes. This is done to ensure that these teachers align with Swedish contextual skills and necessary language skills. Common gaps include mismatches in teaching positions and educational backgrounds between the former and new education systems. Sweden's desire to assimilate migrant teachers reflects its dedication to inclusivity, enriching its educational environment.

The 2018 Migrant World Values Survey (MWVS), spearheaded by Puranen (2019), captured the perspectives of 6,500 migrants from 130 countries. The survey revealed migrants' appreciation for Sweden's education but reservations about its progressive gender equality stance. Many exhibited cultural adaptability. Sweden, as per the World Values Survey, is secular and individualistic. By outlining the fundamental values and tasks of the school, the curriculum expects educators to uphold inclusivity and foster individual responsibility. The teachers' beliefs are intertwined with these values and include a digital competency component. For migrant teachers, the challenge is blending or maintaining the balance between personal beliefs and professional values in the school environment. Migrant teachers want to discuss fundamental values during the bridging programme. However, the challenge of blending personal beliefs with professional values is not exclusive to migrants, especially in a heterogeneous society like Sweden. Sweden has a wide range of ideas; however, for some migrants, this is, to an extent, unfamiliar to bring into a school environment. One interpretation of a pedagogical democratic environment is that the students have a voice and are in the centre of teaching, not the teacher.

A teacher's core beliefs about learning define and steer their teaching style and interactions with students, underpinning their professional identity and teaching methods. Thus, migrant teachers' professional identities are pivotal in professional transitions, moulded by varying contexts. The migrant teacher's professional identities emerge from those prioritising migration experiences, those prioritising pedagogy, and those blending both. Migrant teachers often face adaptation challenges. Projects such as R/EQUAL (Proyer et al., 2019; Terhart et al., 2020) bridge experiences, thereby aiding the integration of migrant teachers.

In the next section, we will look into some research I have done previously and my ongoing research that involves migrant teachers' experiences in Swedish teacher education. I will start with Illeris's theory of redefining transformative learning and identity (2014b, 2017), further Kreber (2009) and Entwistle et al. (2002) ways of thinking and practising in higher education.

As a researcher and teacher educator, I find these theories useful when I design my teaching.

2 Migrant Teachers and Transformative Learning

In this section, I will outline the theoretical framework underpinning my research and my approach to teaching, explicitly focusing on migrant teachers. I intend to revisit findings from my earlier studies on migrant teachers within the context of Swedish teacher education, shedding light on their experiences in a novel educational context. Finally, I will present outcomes from my current research project about migrant teachers.

2.1 What Is Redefined Transformative Learning?

Mezirov (1975, 1978a, 1978b, 1991) created the term transformative learning. Mezirov saw changes in self-perceptions and transformations in meaning perspectives, such as how an individual defines herself and the relationships, when studying women's liberation processes in community college courses. Within transformative learning, qualitative changes are involved in how a person understands herself (the learners' perspectives on meaning) or reference frames (meaning perspectives). Hence, the core of transformative learning is a critical reflection with its results implemented in practice (Mezirov, 1978a, 1991). Illeris, a Danish professor emeritus in lifelong learning, values Mezirow's work on transformative learning but criticises the definition as too narrow and broadens the concept (2014a, 2014b). Illeris defines transformative learning as "learning which implies a change in the learner's identity" (2014a, 2014b, p. 40, 2014c), including three dimensions of learning: cognitive, emotional, and social. Illeris discusses transformative learning in relation to competence development, learning environments, general learning theory, sociology, and psychology (2014a, 2014b). The foundation is that transformative learning is part of everyone's life since we live in a constantly changing society. Hence, all individuals' life conditions and identities change through transformative learning processes (Illeris, 2014b, 2017). He relates to Bauman's liquid modernity and constantly developing societies (Bauman, 2000). Bauman argues that the fluidity of liquid has the quality of being able to change continually and is ready to change, as the opposite of solid. He relates this (liquidity) to the present modernity.

Illeris has mainly worked with adult learning and extensively produced text concerning learning theory. Illeris has different models that are used more empirically: learning triangle (Rosenow-Gerhard, 2021), dual triangular workplace learning model for workplace learning, and identity formation Illeris (2011; Zhao & Ko, 2018). Zhao and Ko (2018) identified that how teachers perceive their professional identity is echoed by how they exercise their agency using their skills in workplace learning. Teachers identify themselves with the work emphasising the significance of workplace learning practices, individual and social aspects of learning situations, and individual and social levels of workplace learning. Illeris (2015) emphasises that transformative learning is only one kind of learning and stresses a distinction between cumulative, assimilative, accommodative, and transformative learning. There are two basic learning processes: the integration of external interaction (learner and the social, cultural, and material environment) and the internal psychological (acquisition and elaboration). He considers learning as any process that leads to permanent capacity change, which involves two processes: (a) interaction (individual and the social and material environment) and (b) the internal elaboration and acquisition of the impulses from the process of interaction (2014a, 2017). However, this acquisition involves the content (what is learned) and the learning incentive (motivation, emotion, volition). It stresses the notion of situated learning, interactive and social, interpreted by the learner (Illeris, 2014b, 2017).

Learning according to redefined transformative learning will be described. First, there is a distinction between learning as an addition (cumulative, when a pattern is already established), assimilative (new things add to what is already known), and change (accommodation). Different types of accommodation are ordinary, in which someone understands something in a new way, accepting what is different, and transformative, in which the learner changes their meaning, perspectives, or actions. Accommodation as transformative learning includes cognitive, emotional, and social dimensions, which change the identity. Interestingly, transformative learning cannot be taught; teacher educators can only strive after it, organise and plan for it, but in the end, it is an individual internal process which is situated. Accordingly, situated learning forms what is learned and how the person relates to what is learned (Illeris, 2004, 2014b, 2015, 2017, 2018). One example is when Wen et al. (2023) studied foreign Western teachers' professional identity and confidence development through transformative learning whilst teaching at a Sino-English University in China (English served as the teaching language). Their pedagogical and curricular rationales underpin the Western teachers' professional identity as educators. Thus, it was through transformative learning and critical reflection on their experiences that they could overcome workplace challenges and gain competencies promoting transnational education. As such, the reflective practice helped teachers develop their identity and confidence in unfamiliar situations (Wen et al., 2023).

Language-associated barriers could be a matter of language proficiency, missing background knowledge, or not knowing the meaning behind the message. Based on transformative learning, the teachers reflected on how to solve problems related to their professional identity. The solution was to become a learning partner and a student helper. The online learning environment forced Western teachers to change perspectives to a more inclusive, differentiated teaching. They constructed online resources and paid more attention to being more accessible to the students in the online environment, helping them develop study habits (Wen et al., 2023). The concept of identity consists of the experience of being an individual in the world who relates to and is experienced by others.

The identity model constructed by Illeris (2014b) has three layers. The inner layer of the model represents the core identity, the experience of being an individual, a relatively stable part of the identity. With its values, understanding, behaviour, communication habits, and collaboration patterns, the personality layer is to be found outside the core. This layer is a common target for transformative learning since it relates to an individual's values and habits that change with new experiences and conditions. Finally, we find the preference layer, which consists of what and how a person prefers, routines, and automatic reactions. This layer is not the primary target for transformative learning since it relates to learning as an addition and not essential to identity. It is important that identity changes by learning throughout one's life (Illeis, 2014b, 2017). The layers are the general identity structure, a central identity relating to a person as a whole. In addition, there is the concept of part-identities or identity areas (Illeris, 2014b). They relate to two main areas: attitudes, which include national-cultural and religious-political part-identity and practice with work, family, and everyday interest part-identities. Some elements in part-identities have great importance, while others are weak since they are part of individual interactions.

Professional work identity is particularly interesting for this Element since it integrates personal identity and working life. For readability in relation to the Element as a whole, professional identity and not work identity will be used. All part-identities are differentiated in a stable core, a more flexible outer layer that changes through transformative learning, and an unstable layer that changes more easily. Illeris mapped a structure of qualification areas to this. Illeris (2014b) argues that an individual defines herself in relation to the work; thus, it is one of the most important part-identities. They can be addressed at different levels: basic, comprehensive, and specific (Illeris, 2014b). Workplace-related qualifications cannot be understood without looking at an individual's development more holistically (Illeris 2014b). Thus, transformative learning can be helpful as a holistic approach in modern liquid society.

Owens (2018) developed a transitional and professional identity development model related to Illeris's identity concept. This is by referring to nurse practitioners' identity development through transformative learning experiences, a currently situated individual learning with a linkage between past learning experiences and interactions individually, which forms what is learned and how the individual relates to this. Owens (2018) states that this model can guide and support nurse practitioners' programmes. The identity transition for family rural nurse practitioners involved incentives to learn (new skills, knowledge, and roles), a passion for working in rural healthcare, and relationships with their patients, colleagues, and stakeholders (Owens, 2018).

It is possible to understand migrant teachers' experience with a new educational context in relation to Illeris' redefined transformative learning theory with its professional identity and authentic competence development (2014c). I will concentrate on the Illeris identity model because it is my experience that migrant teachers reflect on subjects that can be placed within this model. It can be of transformative deep insights related to the core layer or more surface-based themes connected to the preference layer. During seminars, we often discuss issues related to the personality layers. Few empirical articles are based explicitly on Illeris's theory of identity even though they refer to him conceptually (Wen et al., 2023); however, some use the whole identity model (Baldwin & Motter, 2021). A study that uses Illeris' theoretical identity framework as a lens is, for example, Baldwin and Motter's (2021) study of learners in an ethnographic dance course, and findings revealed that one-third of the class experienced a transformed identity during their education. The student utilised choreographic motifs to convey the emotional elements of a personal story, helping them navigate their emotional sensitivity. In research done by Yip (2023), the focus is on the emotion of professional vulnerability experienced by teachers who migrated from Asia to Australia.

In their research, Wen et al. (2023) met Western teachers who wanted to participate and interact with the local Chinese community to understand their social and cultural points of view since it would help them in their teaching. When Western teachers reflected on their experiences during cross-cultural online teaching, particularly during unfamiliar and critical incidents, their professional identity changed, thus transforming their pedagogical and curricular knowledge. During their meaning-making process, new perspectives were revealed, and their identity shifted from class teachers to learning partners (Wen et al., 2023). There are many ways to view and define what competence can be. Is it the precondition for qualification for certain areas or the more general way of providing an individual with a capacity to meet the unknown? For Illeris (2014a), it has to do with the latter; it supports the learner's capability to function in new societal situations. Further, competence related to societal conditions reaches into identity, being conscious, and having the ability to act

(2014a). In order to achieve this, we can talk about a learner-centred approach with authentic competence development that involves transformative learning. To achieve this, the learning has to involve (a) engagement, (b) practice/ problem, and (c) reflection (Illeris, 2014b, 2017). Even though practice is not always an option, working with problem-oriented teaching and learning is possible. This will include more personal involvement, according to Illeris (2015). This transformative practice includes individual experience, critical reflection, dialogue/discussion, holistic orientation (cognitive, emotional, and social), awareness of context (personal and sociocultural conditions), and authentic relationships (especially between teachers and learners) (Taylor, 2009). According to Wen et al. (2023), Western teachers transformed their challenges into expertise for teaching in an online cross-cultural setting. In doing so, their confidence as teachers increased, and a reflective practice also renewed their teaching identities. The transformative learning process facili- tated reflection, enabling them to recognise and instigate change. Consequently, their professional identity evolved, allowing them to reassess their practice within this unfamiliar cultural environment.

Transformative learning is suitable for higher education and is used in project studies. Project studies are one type of way that allows students to relate to their identities and development of competence, more than old-fashioned education since they are provoked to express themselves in a multitude of ways, take a stand in decisions, reflect, and evaluate in relation to tasks, goals, situations, others, and more (Illeris, 2015). However, a transformation is not always progressive; it can be regressive or defensive when the learner feels uncertain or overwhelmed. Unfortunately, this can result in withdrawal, regression, or resignation (Illeris, 2014b). When resistance to learning occurs, it is important to understand why and address it (Illeris, 2014a). Additionally, a way of stimulating intercultural under- standing is to challenge and think critically about one's beliefs and then change, called 'act-change-oriented' learning (Taylor & Cranton, 2012).

2.2 Familiar and Unfamiliar Ways of Thinking and Practising

The ETL project, Enhancing Teaching-Learning Environments in Undergraduate Courses Project, was the first to introduce the theory of 'ways of thinking and practising' (Entwistle, 2003). Ways of thinking and practising can be described as unique traditions and practices essential to education. These ways of thinking and practising can be intuitive, cognitive, tacit, and performative. Students learn some ways of thinking and practising that transcend disciplinary boundaries. While working with tasks in the current habitus, the student teachers develop a feel for tacit ways of thinking and practising. They do not only look at the content but the task through the ways of thinking and practising, habits of thought and practice, which are constantly challenged by reflection (Kreber, 2009). There are several examples in which the different ways of thinking and practising are investigated in a subject. For instance, the ways of thinking and practising in biology substantially impacted the teaching and learning assessment strategies in courses at the biology department (McCune & Hounsell, 2005). Furthermore, Eckerdal (2009) investigated the conceptual and practical learning of novice computer programming students by using ways of thinking and practising.

Even though ways of thinking and practising greatly influence teachers and the activities and strategies they choose, what is taught is not solely subject-specific. Instead, it can make student teachers more familiar with the unfamiliar scholarly communication within a community, which gives them a meta-understanding of the new knowledge. The students learn how to think like a historian or nurse and act as one. Therefore, a specific culture, department, and discipline affect the way teachers teach (Hounsell & Anderson, 2009). The tacit knowledge makes teaching and learning more difficult for teachers and students to comprehend (Meyer & Land, 2003). Consequently, a deeper understanding of ways of thinking and practising increases the possibility of a transformed understanding of knowledge and how students experience something within a discipline or generally (Entwistle et al., 2002; McCune & Reimann, 2002). By developing a deeper understanding of new and unfamiliar ways, students gain tools to handle and interpret other situations (Eatwell et al., 1998). The university teacher has a pedagogical task to aid students in understanding the ways of thinking and practising. This has an essential pedagogical value due to the fact that students put much effort and time into interpreting other teaching models (Meyer & Land, 2003, 2005; Meyer et al., 2010).

The concept of unfamiliar ways of thinking and practising could help study migrant teachers' experiences with teacher education and the Swedish school context. This concept, unfamiliar in relation to ways of thinking and practising that Käck introduced (2019a), carries neither an inherently positive nor negative connotation. It simply denotes something perceived as new, which can be viewed positively, neutrally, or even negatively. This perception varies: while one might find the unfamiliar intriguing or refreshing, another might consider it strange, confusing, or worth avoiding (Käck, 2019). Teachers with migrant backgrounds have learned ways of thinking and practising in their former country. Not only do they have to discover what it means to be a teacher in Sweden and be introduced to Swedish education, but they must also interlink and compare these sometimes new, unfamiliar experiences with their former ways of thinking and practising. The definition of 'unfamiliar ways of thinking and practising' is 'something that is experienced as unknown or unfamiliar in teaching and learning or in what constitutes a profession in a new context' (Käck, 2019a). This definition makes it possible to identify challenges that can appear in a new professional and educational environment. When teachers with a foreign teaching degree discover and compare both familiar and unfamiliar ways of thinking and practising, they can transform their understanding of teaching and how education is practised and understood in, for example, Sweden.

2.3 Attending the Swedish Teacher Education

In this section, I will discuss findings from my earlier research on migrant teachers, framing them within Illeris's theory of identity and focusing particularly on the concept of professional identity (Illeris, 2014b). The migrant teachers I studied had foreign teaching degrees that required at least two years of university-level education. They were also enrolled in supplementary programmes at four Swedish universities. For more profound knowledge about the studies, look into the references (Käck, 2018b; Käck, 2019a, 2019b; Käck, 2020a; Käck, 2020b; Käck et al., 2018a; Käck et al., 2019b). This cohort of migrant teachers corresponds to the same demographic that I encounter and educate, even though I was not acquainted with these specific individuals prior to conducting the research. In the past, I taught a course named To be a Teacher in Sweden 22,5 ECTs; today, I teach them in Special Education 7,5 ECTs every semester.

The research design consisted of convergent mixed methods (Creswell & Plano Clark, 2011, 2017; Venkatesh et al., 2013), combining data collection and analysis from:

a) a web-based survey with 228 migrant teachers with former teacher education in Algeria, Argentina, Azerbaijan, Bangladesh, Belarus, Belgium, Bosnia and Herzegovina, Brazil, Bulgaria, Canada, Central America, Chile, China, Costa Rica, Cuba, Egypt, Ethiopia, Finland, Georgia, Germany, Greece, Hungary, India, Iraq, Iran, Japan, Jordan, Kenya, Kosovo, Kurdistan, Latvia, Lebanon, Lithuania, Mongolia, Netherlands, Nicaragua, Pakistan, Palestine, Philippines, Poland, Romania, Russia, Serbia, Spain, South Africa, Syria, Taiwan, Thailand, Turkey, Ukraine, USA, Uzbekistan, Yugoslavia, and Zambia;

b) nine individual interviews with migrant teachers with former teacher education in Hungary, Latvia, Canada, Nicaragua, Palestine, Philippines, Russia, Serbia, and South Africa;

c) twenty-five migrant teachers in five focus groups with former teacher education in Belarus, Bulgaria, China, Estonia, Hungary, India, Iraq, Iran, Latvia, Mongolia, Peru, Poland, Philippines, Russia, and Ukraine; fifteen migrant teachers submitted personal reflective texts about their teachers' beliefs. They had a former teacher education in the Balkans, Bangladesh, China, Germany, Hungary, Iraq, Iran, Kurdistan, Latvia, Lebanon, Serbia, and Ukraine;

d) thirty reflective texts about teaching beliefs written by fifteen migrant teachers

There are many reasons why migrant teachers come to Sweden; however, they are transitioning to change culture and language upon their arrival. Migrant teachers discussed society and education, focusing specifically on the Swedish system and its values. These values could prove challenging to understand and require time to process. While finding their professional work identity, the inner core of the teacher's role could be very different. They expressed that this society (Sweden) has shared perspectives, specific values, and principles that are taken for granted but can seem contradictory to the former country. 'When I migrated to Sweden, I was in limbo for a year. I did not know who I was; I got problems with my identity.' In Sweden, being a teacher is more akin to being a supervisor, in contrast to countries where the teacher is viewed as an authoritative figure that people look up to. 'I was like a mayor in my former country' (Käck, 2019b). Being treated so differently as a teacher in various countries can be quite shocking. Transitioning from a highly respected position to a role with a significantly reduced status can be jarring. It may mean facing questions from society, parents, and students in ways you're unaccustomed to. Such experiences strike at the very heart of one's professional identity, shaking one's self-perception as a teacher. Some argue that adjusting and determining how to be and act takes considerable time. The topic frequently arises during seminars, with teachers comparing their roles in their home countries to those in Sweden. Furthermore, what if the teaching role in Sweden is not one you desire, and you find yourself longing for the respect your previous position commanded? How does one cope with that? These are the questions that migrant teachers often wish to discuss during the bridging programme.

This led to how migrant teachers sought to comprehend themselves within a broader framework to discern what was expected of them as teachers in a new country. 'I need to immerse myself in the Swedish curriculum, the norms, and values of the society to establish this in the classroom.' 'I encountered lots of problems in the beginning. One needs to understand everything happening in the teacher education and the Swedish school system, how to think and relate to the former teacher education and what you are learning at the Swedish teacher education.' Migrant teachers spoke of a transformed professional identity due to differences in cultural systems, values in the curriculum, and specific competencies related to teaching in Sweden. 'I have gained a lot of competence, the knowledge that I did not have before, for example, how to work democratically, write developing plans for each pupil in class … things that are essential for being a teacher in Sweden.' (Käck et al., 2018a). Some teachers employed digital technologies to process and understand their identities in Sweden, using the Internet to compare now and then. 'I searched the Internet to compare the concept of fundamental values within educational systems [in different countries].' Thus, the teachers wanted to understand the foundation of teaching and learning in Sweden in relation to themselves as teachers and expressed transformative accommodation, changing perspectives and ways of behaving (Käck, 2019b).

Some respondents were familiar with the ways of thinking and practising (Kreber, 2009; Entwistle, 2003) in the Swedish context. However, for other migrant teachers, the transition into the Swedish context was experienced as unfamiliar because of the cultural embeddedness of Swedish teacher education. The unfamiliarity with Swedish teaching practices (Kreber, 2009; Käck, 2018b; Käck et al., 2018a; Käck, 2019b; Käck et al., 2019b) reflects an initial unfamiliarity with the 'values' and 'behaviour' dimensions of their work identity. This suggests a redefined transformative learning experience and an altered teaching perspective (Käck, 2018b; Käck, 2019b; Käck et al., 2019b). The shift from teacher-centred to student-centred teaching (Käck et al., 2018a) indicates a transformation, and for migrant teachers who embraced this, there is a change in meaning and perspective in their work identity. Unfamiliar teaching and learning methods and environments were related to new pedagogical methods, digital technologies, and different ways of acquiring knowledge, for example, independent, student-centred, self-directed learning, group work and using group environments, and social learning. Some were frustrated with the focus on student independence and not on the teacher (Käck et al., 2018a). 'The other thing is how you participate as a teacher-student during the lessons; I was not used to this.' 'It was problematic for me to conform … It took me about a year to get used to and use this way of learning [self-directed, autonomous]. I was very stressed out. You have the former system of doing things within you.' (Käck, 2019b). I heard the same thing from refugee teachers in Germany (R/EQUAL project).

When things were very unfamiliar, it took a year to adjust. Additionally, some of the learning environments and group settings were new, requiring time to adapt. We will revisit this topic later. Approximately 10 per cent of the migrant teachers from fifty-seven countries (as indicated in the web survey) responded that the Swedish teaching and learning environment was very unfamiliar. However, almost everything was familiar to some because migrant teachers constituted a heterogeneous group, and most of them were somewhere in between (Käck et al., 2018a; Käck, 2018b).

It was unfamiliar to some migrant teachers that digital competence was mandated in curricula, laws, and ordinances in society (The National Agency for Education, 2013, 2019, 2022), as well as in the higher education ordinance (Ministry of Education and Research, 2014a). 'The teaching is different [in Sweden]; there are a lot of digital technologies in use that I never had as a teacher-student [former country].' (Käck, 2019b).

The unfamiliarity was due to a lack of infrastructure, money, or restrictions on using digital technologies for citizens in their former countries. 'We did not have digital technology, media, or cell phones because it was forbidden.' 'I come from a poor family, and I understood at the time that in my former country, there were universities that used advanced technology, but that was only for the rich.' In some cases, handwriting was preferred based on teachers' beliefs, attitudes, and practices (Käck, 2018b). Since digital competence is important in the Swedish national curriculum and teacher education, it is a must for migrant teachers to have this knowledge and thus be a part of their competence and work identity. I (2019b) studied migrant teachers' (from fifty-seven countries) self-estimated digital competence according to TPACK (Technological Pedagogical Content Knowledge) (Schmidt et al., 2009) and analysed it in relation to the European framework for digital competence for educators, DigCompEdu (Redecker, 2017), and the European framework for digital competence in general, DigComp 2.1 (Carretero et al., 2017).

Findings revealed a range of competence levels, with some teachers at the foundational level citing reasons like the lack of importance of digital technologies in their prior environments (Käck et al., 2019b). Conversely, others had high proficiency (Pioneers and LeadersDigComp ranking 7–8), were able to solve complex problems, and contributed to professional practice. Some respondents reported a greater integration of digital technologies in their prior education than in Sweden. Further, I (2019c) further explored how technologies were used in Swedish teacher education as well as migrant teachers' former ones. The results showed that digital technologies and their use were higher among placement supervisors and teacher education in Sweden than in their former countries (Käck, 2019b). 'The teachers (in Sweden) do everything using digital technology and media: results, grades, assignments, lessons, explanations, contact with parents, etc.' (Käck, 2018b). The personality layer (Illeris, 2014a, 2014b, 2014c), which encompasses values, behaviour, and collaboration patterns, presents elements of unfamiliarity for some migrant teachers. They expressed this unfamiliarity regarding digital communication, collaboration, and socialisation within the relationships between teachers, educators, and migrant teachers (Käck, 2019b).

Based on the results, migrant teachers indicated that they were unfamiliar with certain examination methods, such as blended examinations (including oral, technology-based, and group examinations), feedback methods, and the promotion of process and formative assessment (as opposed to solely focusing on the results and summative aspects). It could be a clash about how to write exams; for some, questioning the literature or what the teacher educator taught is forbidden. Those migrant teachers said they had to adapt to the teacher educator's conclusions in their writing; otherwise, it could lead to lower grades. On the contrary, in Sweden, if the student teacher does not write critically their reflections, they receive a lower grade (Käck et al., 2018a). 'Here [in Sweden] we have group examinations ... In country X, we had lectures, read the book and then an examination.' '(Strange) that the development process is more important than the result [in Sweden].' 'In country X, we had a lot of written assignments that we handed to the teacher. Here [in Sweden] you have so many group rooms so you can discuss in groups and present to the teacher. I never did that in country X.' (Käck et al., 2018a). There were migrant teachers who expressed how working in groups was included both in school and in their teacher education. Others had neither worked in groups in school nor in their teacher education. 'This was new for me. We never worked in groups in compulsory school nor at the university.' 'They expressed group work as problematic before they learned how to work with it.' 'In country X, you do not discuss in groups. The teacher conveys knowledge in the form of a lecture.' ' ... strange with much group work and discussion.' (Käck et al., 2018a). 'Social learning could be interesting, "Interesting insights for me were the learning connected to social aspects.'.

However, autonomous, student-centred teaching was rejected by some migrant teachers both in teacher education and in schools (Käck, 2019b). 'The teacher walks in, writes something on the board, and lets the pupils work in groups independently. What kind of education is that? As a teacher, you are a well of knowledge to students. You have to fill them up ... " (Käck, 2018b). There was some criticism of these teaching methods, with certain migrant teachers expressing a preference for teacher-centred teaching and missing its absence (Käck et al., 2018a). The transition from teacher-centred to student-centred teaching posed the most significant challenge (Käck, 2018b). My experience teaching migrant teachers indicated a shift in classroom dynamics. They felt this shift was particularly evident in their teaching at the personality layer.

Both positive and negative attitudes toward the new and unfamiliar were expressed, and migrant teachers had to negotiate if the new ways of thinking and practising were something they wanted to have as part of their work identity (Käck, 2018b; Käck et al., 2018a). Since migrant teachers are a heterogeneous group, they have diverse experiences. This was also evident in teacher education, and migrant teachers talked about the unfamiliar expectations of the relationships and roles between them and teacher educators, which took time and energy to understand and seemed culturally determined (Käck et al., 2018a). Thus, for some, the teacher educators were unapproachable authorities, not to be questioned, or the teacher educators in the former country stepped into their private sphere. In Sweden, the teacher educator (or to be a teacher in the school) is seen more as a guide or a mentor than an authoritative central figure. 'The teacher's work (in Sweden) is to guide you somehow, not teach you directly, help you look for knowledge, or put knowledge directly in your head. Here, it is much more up to the student's responsibility.' 'As a student, I want to have someone who says that now you should read these pages, someone who has control, here it is more independent,' ' ... to not have someone that is in charge and deciding over me, that is what feels tricky sometimes' (Käck et al., 2018a). 'In country X I struggled to achieve the level of knowledge that the teacher educator demanded. Here [in Sweden], you struggle with the knowledge itself, not the information that the teacher demands.' 'The teaching is different [in Sweden]; you are expected to partici-pate much more in the teaching, as a student. I am not used to this.' 'It was strange to me that a teacher-student was expected to be so independent when searching for and processing knowledge. You have to obtain this way of learning, to work with the knowledge and the education yourself.' (Käck et al., 2018a).

As can be seen, migrant teachers try to figure out the relationship between them and the teacher educator. The expectations of how the teacher educator should act and teach varied. In my teaching, I know when I walk into a room filled with migrant teachers, this is the span I must understand and act upon. Some of the migrant teachers want me to be that authoritative figure; others will think that the teacher educator in their former country stepped more into their personal sphere than the Swedish one. I have to express what is to be expected in our relationship.

Of utmost importance and much appreciated by migrant teachers was the placement time, being in an authentic learning environment (Käck, 2018b). The placement period was vital in their transformative learning journey since the authentic environment facilitated changes in their values, understanding, behav-iour, and communication habits, thus supporting the development of a new work identity. This relates to Taylor's (2009) core elements of conducting transformative practice: critical reflection, individual experience, context awareness, dialogue/ discussion, and authentic relationships. This was crucial for their professional identity development. The placement supervisor acted as a mediator and guide, helping them bridge their past experiences with the new ones and interlinking their beliefs from their former educational context with the Swedish one. The goal is not to turn teachers with migrant backgrounds into Swedish teachers. Instead, a new professional identity will emerge, making the teachers feel more comfortable and thrive in a new teaching and learning context (Käck, 2018b). Migrant teachers expressed that the placement time gave them a deeper, more insightful understanding of teaching roles and processes (Käck, 2018b).

Migrant teachers expressed uncertainty about an unfamiliar environment and a lack of confidence in intercultural skills. 'The fear -How will I feel like a teacher in a school in another culture, another country?' However, this was solved during the placement period. 'The teaching role (in Sweden) is completely different, so now that I have done all the placement, it is easier for me to adapt my whole situation to how things are in Sweden. Now I work the way I was taught at the placement.' 'I had such an amazing supervisor. She understood how everything worked, how to talk to colleagues, how to talk to students, how to behave around colleagues and students, how to look . . . she was perfect.' (Käck, 2018b). The results indicated the cultural embeddedness of Swedish education, showing how migrant teachers struggle with unfamiliar teaching and learning methods, epistemological differences, examination practices and the roles and expectations between teachers and students. However, the placement period proved invaluable for their authentic competence development (Käck et al., 2018a).

The preference layer of the identity (Illeris, 2014a, 2014b, 2014c) concerns what an individual prefers, such as routines, with learning as addition or assimilation. One example is that digital technologies are used for routine work, information, and administration, not demanding deeper processing or identity change from the user, and are often perceived as something good. However, it could also be seen as a negative for learning and a waste of time (Käck, 2019b). Regressive transformative learning was identified (Käck, 2019b) when migrant teachers perceived themselves as digitally illiterate or felt unfamiliar with certain new pedagogical approaches. It was stressful for them when both technologies and pedagogy were unfamiliar. Migrant teachers also wanted to know ordinary basic things in school to collaborate with colleagues seamlessly (Käck, 2019). The dynamics at the preference layer should not be underestimated. Migrant teachers emphasise their desire to know fundamental things, such as placing chairs on the benches at the end of the school day or dressing appropriately for preschool. According to the migrant teachers, nothing can be too simple. For instance, a preschool teacher from a multimillion city recounted arriving at a Swedish preschool in sandals and a skirt, only to discover her Swedish colleagues clad in boots, prepared to accompany the children to the forest to dig up worms in the mud. Even though superficial, the lack of this knowledge was expressed as frustrating by migrant teachers.

Now we will continue with my current research project, 'Bridging programme for teachers educated abroad, the teacher's identity, and teaching philosophy. Migrant teachers' re-contextualization of their teaching profession.' (2022–2025, Utlandsutbildade lärares vidareutbildning, läraridentitet och pedagogiska grundsyn. Utlandsutbildade lärares re-kontextualisering av sin lärarprofession i mötet med ett annat lands utbildningskontext.).

2.4 Migrant Teachers' Redefined Identity

2.4.1 The Study Background

When I was asked to write this element, I wanted to get some new research information and insights from migrant teachers from my present research study (2022–2025), and you will find it here in Section 2.4. Together with my colleague Larissa Mickwitz, senior lecturer at the Department of Education, Stockholm University, we wrote an extensive application to The Swedish Ethical Review Authority, which was approved (Dnr 2022–02211–01), and all ethical formalities were attained; furthermore, the ethical recommendations of the Swedish Research Council (Hermerén, 2017) were followed. I reached out to the National Coordinator for the Bridging Programme for Teachers Educated Abroad at Stockholm University, Susanna Malm, who brought this to the national steering group. Participants in this steering group informed migrant teachers via their information sites at six universities. Migrant teachers were asked to contact me directly if they were interested in participating in this research study, and those who did this came from four Swedish universities. We gathered focus groups and interviewed them. In the present study, Mickwitz contributed by conducting interviews with me. Six focus groups with eighteen migrant teachers gathered in May and June 2022. They got their former teacher's degree from Bulgaria, Chile, Dubai, Iran, Iraq, Kurdistan/Iraq, Lithuania, Mexico, Pakistan, Russia, Syria, Thailand and Vietnam. Eleven were still attending the supplementary education 'Bridging Programme for Teachers Educated Abroad', whereas seven were alumni.

The research question for this present study was: Who am I as a teacher in Sweden, a new country? The study will discuss the findings in relation to the Illeris transformative model of identity (Illeris, 2014a, 2014b, 2014c, 2017) and ways of thinking and practising, familiar or unfamiliar (Entwistle, 2003; Kreber, 2009; Käck, 2019a), which are described earlier in this Element (Sections 2.1 and 2.2). These frameworks informed the study in the analysis of the results and discussion.

The semi-structured interviews were recorded and lasted between 63 and 78 minutes. The strength of the focus group interview is that it was possible to discuss their experiences in Swedish teacher education and compare them to their former teacher education; thus, they listened and reflected on the other's experiences. Focus groups are useful when investigating experiences (Bryman, 2012; Cousin, 2009). Except for the interviews that Mickwitz and I conducted together, the rest of the present study was done by me. All interviews were transcribed verbatim, and qualitative thematic data analysis was conducted using the software program version MAXQDA2020. The data was read through several times for familiarisation, followed by coding with the question 'Who am I as a teacher in a new country?' in mind. Units of meaning for similarities and differences were identified. A total of 311 codes were identified. First, the context appeared and was used as the main themes: Society, Supplementary Education, and Workplace. The themes and sub-themes will be presented next. For ethical reasons, the eleven migrant teachers still attending the supplementary education are called MT1-11 in the quotations, whereas seven were alums and are called MTA12-18. Four men and fourteen women participated.

2.4.2 Findings

The first theme, 'Society', encompasses the sub-themes 'Laws and Regulations', 'Curriculum and Values', and 'Professional Identity'. Here, migrant teachers articulate their experiences of being educators in a new societal context, delving into the nuances of new laws and regulations, the curriculum, and its fundamental values and school-related tasks. The second theme, 'Supplementary Education', comprises sub-themes such as 'Facilitating Transformative Learning', 'Identity Negotiation and Finding Balance', focusing on their experiences within teacher education programmes. The third theme, 'Workplace', relates to how migrant teachers connect their professional identity with their work environment. This theme includes sub-themes like 'Belonging, Trust, and Collaboration', 'Reflections on Teaching Practice', and 'Strengths and Challenges Regarding Language', addressing their relational dynamics and linguistic experiences in the workplace. They were concerned with relationships with students, colleagues, and parents and how the language connected or separated them from the students. Migrant teachers reflected on familiar and unfamiliar methods and created new strategies to handle the old and new. Given the heterogeneity of migrant teachers, the themes and sub-themes span a spectrum from unfamiliar to familiar, encapsulating diverse facets of their professional journey. These reflect which layers in Illeris's identity model were impacted and worked with individually. Analysing the results in the context of transformative learning, transformative identity, and the identity layers proposed by Illeris offers an understanding of the changes and adaptations migrant teachers undergo.

Society

Laws and Regulations

Migrant teachers highlighted the importance and necessity of understanding Swedish schools' history, laws, and regulations to grasp the educational landscape. Moreover, it is necessary to understand the current situation. They desired deeper knowledge to feel secure during in-service, practice, or work sessions, seeking guidance on appropriate student interaction and communication with parents, which indicates a change in the learner's identity in relation to emotional and social dimensions of redefined transformative learning. 'I am so happy that I have so much from the program with me; how can I respond to them (students and parents) with documents about that purpose . . . presenting the governing documents if there is anything.' (MTA12) Consequently, laws and regulations are linked to the personality layer, as they align with aspects of values and behaviour (Illeris, 2014b). Migrant teachers integrate them as part of their professional identity and implement them into practice. The strong focus on students' rights and emphasis on the individual made them uncertain. 'What rights do I have in this situation? Sometimes you get lost and do not know who is right in this situation, the student or me?' (MT4). The emotional tuning to a new cultural and professional environment is coupled with the challenge of establishing social connections. This transformation encompasses managing personal emotions such as insecurity and navigating the novel social dynamics within the workplace. This aspect of transformation is deeply intertwined with cognitive changes, reflecting Illeris's holistic view of learning as an integrative process encompassing multiple dimensions of learning (Illeris, 2014a, 2014b, 2014c).

Curriculum and Values

The school's curriculum, fundamental values, and tasks could be unfamiliar since there were sometimes other perceptions of the school system. Values often emerge as a central topic in focus group interviews with migrant teachers, linking to the personality layer in the Illeris identity model (Illeris, 2014b). For some, the Swedish values are unfamiliar (Käck, 2019a). 'In the beginning, when you read the basics of values, it is very interesting . . . it's like a process . . . face challenges all the time when you start work.' (MT7). Some migrant teachers originate from countries characterised by pronounced hierarchical systems, including dictatorships. 'I think this education (supplementary program) was necessary . . . coming from a dictatorship country. . . . people here (in Sweden) have learned democracy . . . and I learned that the children already, from the age of 1, start to learn the basic values in the preschool in the curriculum . . . it is very important to know.' (MT7). Ways of thinking and practising, the unique traditions, and practices essential to education can be intuitive, cognitive, tacit, and performative (Entwistle, 2003); the students can develop a feel for them working with tasks in the current habitus (Kreber, 2009). The interpretation of the curriculum can vary; in some countries, it is closely linked to the scholars who develop teaching aids and textbooks, which teachers and students follow meticulously from cover to cover. Comparatively, the Swedish curriculum is thin, and you can choose your own teaching aids. The course plan is already determined in our former country. Materials, teaching aids, everything is already decided ... We (teachers) are mediators ... this is a big difference from Sweden ... you are so free to pick, choose and decide as a teacher.' (MT2). Migrant teachers express how they look at content and the task through thinking and practising, constantly challenged by reflection.

Professional Identity

Migrant teachers often face difficulties establishing and gaining recognition for their professional identity, especially when confronted with challenges related to obtaining certification or acknowledging their previous teaching experience. The relatively low status of teachers in Sweden came as a surprise or even a shock to many. Furthermore, their status, specifically as native language teachers, was perceived to be even lower. 'I was shocked ... Whatever title you have, they will call you by your first name; it does not matter ... That was the first shock, and it's called culture clash.' (MT1). The societal perception of one's role as a teacher significantly impacts the core layer of one's identity; it targets the individual holistically (Illeris, 2014b), particularly when there is a substantial disparity, as described by many migrant teachers. Migrant teachers engage in a complex process of identity negotiation, reconciling their past experiences with the new cultural and educational norms. This negotiation is a core aspect of transformative identity, as it involves reconciling different aspects of their self-concept and professional role within a new context. It is not only the name but also how you are seen; you must process how to deal with it.

Supplementary Education

Facilitate Transformative Learning

The bridging programme for teachers educated abroad serves as a supplementary programme, offering migrant teachers the opportunity to familiarise themselves with their new country's educational system. They know everything about teacher work in their former country; however, they describe the programme as discovering a new world with other perspectives. Even routine aspects of Swedish teacher education can be unfamiliar territory. Migrant teachers may face challenges and barriers to engaging in transformative learning, such as language barriers, and would benefit from support in managing those. 'You cannot feel accepted in a group as a foreign teacher. It is not that those whose mother tongue is Swedish do not want to accept us, but sometimes . . ., they do not understand what you say' (MT5). They also talked about a lack of cultural awareness from teacher educators and intercultural education for themselves. They thought Sweden was more multicultural, and 'the cultural knot' needed to be addressed more extensively to understand different cultures in Sweden. This approach would assist them in contextualising their knowledge and adopting a global perspective. 'I dared to open up in front of my case manager . . . the cultural concepts, or cultural knot that I have no idea about . . . like when football teams play a match . . . When I listen to the audience, I understand what they are saying but do not understand it. I understand what that means, but I do not get this under . . . the subcultural stuff . . . I have to work on it. Continuously.' (MT1).

Another aspect addressed the lack of knowledge from the teacher educators about the supplementary course and migrant teachers. 'You can see on their (teacher educators) faces that it becomes a question mark if you say that I am a student in this program . . . . it is better that teachers should know a little before . . . about the program, what kind of background migrant teachers have, and why they are currently studying those courses.' (MT4). Migrant teachers felt they had other questions they wanted to process during their supplementary programme. '(wish) that we would discuss our own case . . . what have you met at school. Swedish students and non-Swedish students. What was the challenge for you when you set the grade, when you met multicultural classes, when you had students with some diagnoses, in relation to parents, how did you meet parents, colleagues, mentors, and the principal . . . different questions, which one has. I feel that there is no room for our own questions, so.' (MT3). What migrant teachers ask for is authentic competence development that targets deeper layers in their work identity. Also, the course literature could be more adapted to their supplementary course. 'Courses have not been adapted to those of us who have a foreign background.' (MT4).

Furthermore, they wanted to learn more about teaching in digital environments since Swedish teachers use it a lot. 'Here you learn a lot . . . to teach, different with the help of different programs and the like . . . I feel stressed . . . when I come to work, and the other teachers know a lot of stuff like that . . . So, all that is new to me, so it would be good if someone could guide me.' (MT7). 'The problem was that we do not have internet in schools . . . not computers in schools, but here in Sweden, it is possible to use projects, show films, and listen to little fairy tales through film . . . Which were almost new methods for me.' (MT8).

Migrant teachers describe and emphasise in-service practice as extremely important. However, they emphasised the experiences they bring into the Swedish school context. Some came from colonial countries and could talk about these experiences from a different perspective than Swedish teachers. These varied experiences and perspectives contribute competencies and insights to the school that would be unattainable without the input of migrant teachers. Some migrant teachers discussed the oral tradition as much more important than written texts. 'It is also completely different from other countries. So, for me, it was quite decisive to have the supplementary education.' (MT3). 'I understood that actually that it is needed (the supplementary program) . . . as you say, it is a completely different context . . . we will work in.' (MT5).

Identity Negotiation and Finding Balance

Migrant teachers may face challenges in maintaining their teacher identities while adapting and navigating a new cultural school environment. They are replacing their old identities with new ones and creating a professional identity with additional skills. This process involves integrating elements of their original teaching identities with new perspectives and practices gained in Sweden. It is a complex, ongoing negotiation that balances respect for their roots with the requirements of the new context, exemplifying the transformative nature of identity as outlined by Illeris. Striking a balance between the old and the new is a complex process. 'When you were a student yourself, then you have the habit of understanding and interpreting signals and knowing about consequences based on what the teacher says . . . Here in Sweden, it does not work at all . . . However, it is still difficult for me for a very long period.' (MT10). To fit in and succeed in new work environments, you need to be aware of your professional identity and its values, the core identity, which is an experience of being an individual, a relatively stable part of the identity. Migrant teachers talk about creating their own professional identity through adaptation, balancing 'former and now' by variation, comparing, finding differences and similarities, observing, and developing. This is a great asset to embrace in teacher education. Adapting to Swedish schools' different roles and expectations signifies a redefinition of their professional identity. This redefinition, often involving a shift from a more authoritative to a more collaborative role, is a prime example of transformative work identity. In some cases, the shift from teacher-centred to student-centred paradigms, or the incorporation of digital technologies, represents more than just a methodological change. It reflects a fundamental shift in how migrant teachers view education, the teacher's role, and the learning process's nature. This shift is at the heart of transformative work identity, challenging and changing core beliefs and values about their profession (Illeris, 2014b).

Workplace

Belonging, Trust, and Collaboration

Migrant teachers may struggle to find a sense of belonging in their new environment. This includes collaboration and teamwork, where they may navigate complex intercultural relationships with colleagues, students, and parents, impacting their sense of identity and belonging. Trust and treatment were keywords for migrant teachers concerning the dean and colleagues. Their self-esteem rose when a dean showed trust by employing them. However, they expressed a need for deeper understanding and knowledge about collegial collaboration. 'Well, okay, the school teaches how to teach. But school never teaches me what to do to be a good colleague.' (MT10). Thus, migrant teachers may need support to build new professional networks. 'Collaboration and the discussion with colleagues is something that can function as support for us who come from other contexts.' (MT5). Communication and collaboration patterns are part of the personality layer and are part of transformative learning (Illeris, 2014b). This is not an easy process; some can be perceived or treated differently due to their migration status or cultural background, and they talk about trust and more knowledge from Swedish teachers both in teacher education and schools. 'The teacher does not know much about you, ... then there is less trust and confidence in you, and they know not exactly what you have with you in your luggage, both from experience in your home country and here in Sweden. So it will be challenging.' (MTA14). For some, the multicultural school environment is new, coming from a more homogenous context, and support was asked for on how to teach in these settings. 'In country x, the context is very homogeneous. So that does not help me (in Sweden).' (MT5).

Social relations, new attitudes, and relations are something many migrant teachers process and reflect on. The relations with students, parents, and colleagues can be different than in their former country. Migrant teachers expressed that during in-service, they were much appreciated when a conflict appeared. They said that the parents of newly arrived students would not accept parts of the Swedish system and talked about themselves as a bridge between the students, parents, and the school, being able to explain the unfamiliarity to them and explain the Swedish system, the laws, curriculum, homework, and responsibility. However, they encounter challenges with more horizontal leadership structures. In the classroom. 'So I'm constantly trying to, you know, develop my leadership tools, actually to control it.' (MT2). Although this transformation is challenging, it offers a unique perspective and understanding of others that Swedish teachers might not possess. Migrant teachers could help newly arrived students as they did not understand the Swedish teacher–student role, which had different responsibilities than in former countries. 'In the former country, we see on a scale of 10, the teacher had the responsibility 8 or 9. The students had the responsibility of only 1 or 2. However, here (in Sweden), it is; I cannot say it is the other way around, but, in any case, it is half, five teachers, five students. This means that the students have a great responsibility here to develop themselves.' (MT1). However, there are some misconceptions about what can be done in a classroom. 'Then there was a student who sat in the chair and had his legs up on . . . on the table . . . . But then I realised that this student is responsible . . . we cannot do anything about it.' (MT1). Adapting and reflecting on teaching approaches based on classroom experiences demonstrates a cognitive and practical transformation in their professional practice. However, classroom dynamics must be transparent and openly discussed, especially when there's a risk of misinterpretation, as highlighted in the previous example. Thus, a mentor would be of utmost importance. Even though the curricula emphasise listening to the students in school, they must follow common classroom rules. The interplay of new cultural norms, societal expectations, and professional standards deeply influences the personality layer. Migrant teachers' responses to these influences involve adapting their external behaviours and internalising new values and norms, which become part of their professional ethos. This internalisation process is critical to understanding this layer's transformation depth.

Reflections on the Teaching Practice

Migrant teachers engage in reflective practice, adjusting their teaching approaches based on classroom experiences. 'And I was almost like an observer. So I observed how they talk to children, how they treat them . . . I found some similarities and differences, tried to compare, and found a balance . . . But slowly, stay still, breathe deeply, observe, and evolve.' (MTA13). Migrant teachers experience cognitive dissonance as they encounter new educational norms and practices. This dissonance can be a critical catalyst in transformative learning, prompting a re-evaluation and reconstruction of their pedagogical understanding. It's not merely about learning new content; it's about reconciling and integrating these new learnings with their pre-existing knowledge and experiences, which is central to Illeris's theory (Illeris, 2014). Migrant teachers talk about adapting to new teaching approaches to fit the educational context. Special needs education and the responsibility to identify and work with these students with different teaching and learning methods are new for some migrant teachers. 'But we learned nothing about special education courses (former country). Which are very, very important ... I had no idea, to be honest, about, for example, what ADHD (attention-deficit/hyperactivity disorder) is, and everything else ... but I still did not know how to work here in Sweden, so it was good that we had this course.' (MT7). 'It is very difficult to work as a teacher in Sweden because you have to think about 20 whole students at the same time ... So it takes time and energy to make customised material for 24 students sitting in the classroom.' (MT4). This is interesting since some of the migrant teachers express that they are used to have over 40 students in each class in their former country.

Additionally, migrant teachers bring innovative methods for teaching and learning from their former country. 'I think the way of working we have used in country x, you teach mathematics, is better than here (in Sweden) ... And we have had good results in country x, better than here.' (MTA8). 'I try to use what I already have, for example, in the subject of mathematics ... But I would love to show my own ... both solution methods on the board. Divide the board and show the two different methods. So in that way ... get a new solution method and show my old solution method to my students.' (MT4).

Of pedagogical interest, migrant teachers develop new approaches and various coping strategies to manage the challenges they face in relation to their new country based on their experiences. 'I learned a lot of new methods and materials here in Sweden, so it was different from country x, and it really helped me a lot ... I teach English in a slightly different way than in the former country.' (MT8). Migrant teachers also had to create their own strategies in order to handle the old and the new. 'In the beginning, I ran the old system as I could ... I could not get out of this myself the first year I started teaching my mother tongue. So I bought a whole set of books ... Do you understand? I created my own ... box. I mean this framework that I have learned to follow. And it gave me time to realise that I am free. I can use another book or no book or ... I do not have to use this one I do not completely agree with ... I slipped out of it steadily.' (MT2).

For instance, they noted a preference for their former country's more transparent assessment system, which they perceived as superior. 'That is how you grade here in Sweden; it is completely different from my home country.' (MT7). Sweden has a vaguer system that demands a lot of preparation; the assessment matrixes are vague, with qualitative versus quantitative ways of assessing. In the former country, it was more controlled and guided. You used textbooks written by researchers/scholars and followed them. 'And because I had such a hard time with this (Swedish) grading system, which was very qualitative, and because I came from a context where the grades were always quantitative, I found a solution where I included just both or some quantitative evidence when grading ... Because you are used to a progression of knowledge, which I did not understand at the beginning either. So, I had to adapt both ways of working a little, with the help of counting.' (MTA18). These are two examples of transformative learning. They start with former ways of thinking and practising, merge them into something in between, and then adapt to a new way. In this case, there is a transformation in the personality layer of the identity. Teacher educators cannot teach this; they only provide learning environments where it can happen. It is an individual process. Post-graduation, migrant teachers express a desire for mentorship – someone to accompany and guide them, allowing them to observe and participate in a typical school day, developing the subject-specific and pedagogical language in Sweden to be able to discuss and understand. 'I had a great mentor ... and presented what you do, what you say, how you react to, to what they say. How to collaborate with colleagues, yes.' (MT10). ". . . how they say this, how they make eye contact . . . You know, the kind of tips that I get, and try to create my own identity.' (MT). Even seemingly minor details, such as students needing to place chairs on the benches before leaving, are aspects migrant teachers wish to learn. 'Not only educational ... example, but all chairs must also be set up. I did not know ... so I wrote it down.' (MT8). Even though this is the surface-based preference layer, it is still something asked for to feel comfortable in a new educational setting. A lot of administrative things were unfamiliar to them; they were delegated to others in their former country. 'Yes, that, the biggest difference is that here in Sweden, I am not just a teacher ... (in my former country) we only teach.' (MT4).

The preference layer, despite being considered a more superficial aspect of identity, unveils the complex dynamics involved in the adaptation process of migrant teachers. This layer covers practical preferences and routines essential for comfort in a new educational setting. The desire for mentorship, understanding of administrative routines, or the tacit knowledge of every day sources reflects deeper needs for security, belonging, and competence in their new roles. These preferences are not just about comfort or convenience; they are integral to the migrant teachers feeling empowered and capable in their new environment, thus impacting a deeper layer in the identity model.

Strengths and Challenges Regarding Language

Migrant teachers may encounter language barriers or other difficulties that impact their work. However, these challenges can also manifest as strengths, as migrant teachers contribute unique linguistic diversity, perspectives, and skills to their teaching and an understanding of how to navigate language barriers and cultural differences in a multilingual classroom. Migrant teachers highlighted language skills, including mastery of school-specific vocabulary and the ability to discuss pedagogical issues with colleagues in discussions. Understanding the system becomes easier during the in-service period, and they stress the importance of mastering language first, as it facilitates the mediation of knowledge. 'And when I read religion (subject), I was happy ... I know Islam. But when I started reading about Islam, I could not understand anything. It was like it was brand new ... different word was used there ... all subjects have their own language, so that is important.' (MT7). Experiencing misunderstandings and diminished respect from students due to less-than-perfect Swedish was stressful and hindered relationship-building. Moreover, understanding students' colloquial 'street language' was challenging for migrant teachers who were more accustomed to academic Swedish. Migrant teachers noted that newly arrived students in compulsory schools often felt more comfortable with them, appreciating the guidance they offered in navigating life in Sweden. 'Guiding if the student has questions . . . . So, there is a big difference. Which confuses most of the newly arrived students.' (MTA15). Following this presentation of new findings, I will proceed to discuss these findings further and explore the pedagogical implications they entail.

2.4.3 Discussion and Pedagogical Implications

Migrant Teachers and the Swedish Education

The analysis of migrant teachers through the lens of Illeris's transformative learning and redefined identity reveals a complex, multifaceted journey for those who experience the Swedish professional identity as unfamiliar. However, every teacher in the world is going through a transformative journey through their lives. As previously mentioned, a broad spectrum ranges from familiar to unfamiliar experiences among migrant teachers (Käck, 2019a; Kreber, 2009). Migrant teachers are not merely acquiring new knowledge and skills adapted to the Swedish context; they are undergoing a transformation through learning that encompasses cognitive, emotional, and social dimensions. The process reflects a dynamic interplay of internal and external factors, leading to a change in their professional identity and practice. This is a sensitive learning experience, and as Kwee (2020) identified, it makes them vulnerable for a very long time.

Of pedagogical interest is that ways of thinking and practising can be described as unique traditions and practices which affect the way teachers teach; students learn some ways of thinking and practising that transcend disciplinary boundaries. While working with tasks, they develop a feel for tacit ways of thinking and practising, not only the content but also constantly challenged by reflection (Entwistle, 2003; Kreber, 2009). However, tacit knowledge makes teaching and learning more difficult for teachers and students to comprehend (Meyer & Land, 2003). Thus, a deeper understanding of ways of thinking and practising increases the possibility of a transformed understanding of knowledge and how students experience something (Entwistle et al., 2002; McCune & Reimann, 2002). This research can help teacher educators to make their teaching for migrant teachers more transparent and design for learning at a deeper level.

When migrant teachers have their former ways of doing things as a starting point, merge them with the new after a while, and embrace new ways of doing things, it is a sign of transformative learning. This was the case within this present study when planning the curriculum and teaching and assessing subjects. Ways of thinking and practising may be familiar or unfamiliar (Entwistle, 2003; Kreber, 2009; Käck, 2019a), but they have to be highlighted and planned for in teacher education to avoid regressive transformation where the learning feels overwhelmed or defensive. Illeris (2014b, 2017) emphasises that competence has to do with the learner's capability to function in new societal situations, linking competence and identity. An authentic learning practice involves engagement, problem-solving, and reflection. Such practices have been particularly effective in higher education settings (Entwistle, 2013; Krever, 2009). As Kelchtermans (2009) states, teachers develop their own interpretative framework, a personal lens, during their studies and practice. Thus, this interpretative framework changes during a teacher's lifetime and is a personal journey. Hence, they highlight their competence as a source of knowledge to be shared in courses and programmes. Teacher educators have a responsibility to facilitate migrant teachers' comprehension of ways of thinking and practising in the new educational context (Meyer & Land, 2003, 2005; Meyer et al., 2010), which can provide invaluable insights into their journey in teacher training and adapting to the educational environment in Sweden (Käck, 2019).

In the findings, migrant teachers describe their experiences in the supplementary education they receive in the context of Swedish teacher education. They are an extremely heterogeneous group; for some, the Swedish teacher education and the school environment are pretty similar; however, they can be unfamiliar for others. Thus, there is a disparity in educational needs among them.

Positive Aspects of Migrant Teachers' Experiences in Swedish Teacher Education

Cultural and Educational Enrichment by Contribution to Educational Diversity

There are several pedagogical implications for working with migrant teachers centred around supporting their transformative learning journey and integrating their diverse experiences. One significant point is acknowledging and recognising the diverse cultural, educational, and professional backgrounds of migrant teachers. The presence of migrant teachers in the Swedish educational system introduces a broad spectrum of teaching perspectives and methodologies, significantly augmenting the cultural richness and inclusivity of the learning environment. The diversity of migrant teachers' backgrounds contributes significantly to the Swedish educational system. The narrative underscores the necessity of an education system that is sensitively attuned to the cultural intricacies of migrant teachers, advocating for an inclusive and comprehensive pedagogical approach by the teacher educators at Swedish teacher education. This diversity, however, is not just a matter of different teaching styles; it represents a broader spectrum of worldviews and educational philosophies, leading to a more globally aware and inclusive educational environment.

The consequential impact of this diversity is evident in students' exposure to varied perspectives and the promotion of enhanced cultural competency among both students and faculty. A pivotal aspect of this engagement involves acknowledging and recognising the rich cultural, educational, and professional tapestry that migrant educators bring to the fore. The narrative thus highlights the imperative for an education system that is finely attuned to the cultural nuances of migrant teachers, advocating for an inclusive and comprehensive pedagogical framework for teacher education. Puranen (2019) could identify how values change among migrants when they move to Sweden compared to individuals in their former country. This is of interest since the curricula constitute a value base in Sweden (The National Agency for Education, 2013, 2019, 2022; Ministry of Education and Research, 2011, 2014a). This influences how the teachers should act and teach in mandatory school and teacher education, working with social learning, being independent and taking responsibility for their learning (Ministry of Education and Research, 1992, 2014a).

Migrant teachers' experiences lead to the development of their professional identity, enriched by adapting to, sometimes, new pedagogical contexts and educational values. The success of this adaptation can be attributed to their resilience and commitment to professional growth, a factor crucial in the integration into diverse educational systems. This transformation is multifaceted, encompassing cognitive, emotional, and social dimensions. The success of this adaptation is attributable to their flexibility and commitment to professional enhancement, which is critical for their integration into diverse educational systems.

Collaborative and Reflective Learning Environments

The interplay of experiences between Swedish and migrant educators engenders a milieu of mutual learning and understanding, catalysing a synergistic effect in the educational landscape. The exchange of experiences between migrant and Swedish educators fosters a collaborative learning environment. This synergy enhances the overall educational landscape with mutual understanding and professional enhancement. This stresses the importance of inclusive pedagogy that respects and incorporates the cultural identities of migrant teachers, promoting a more dynamic and understanding educational environment, and acknowledges the role of teacher educators in facilitating migrant teachers' adaptation, which can provide invaluable insights into their journey and contribute positively to teacher training.

The establishment of collaborative, supportive environments where migrant and Swedish teachers can exchange knowledge and experiences is pivotal. According to the findings, migrant teachers struggle to find a sense of belonging. This is also found in research from other countries as well (Kwee, 2023; Masoumi & Noroozi, 2023; Yan, 2021). The research underscores the mutual benefits of such collaborative learning for Swedish teacher education and mandatory schooling. Collaborative learning can lead to mutual growth and understanding and is beneficial for both Swedish teacher education and mandatory schools. If possible, create a supportive community for migrant teachers where they can share challenges, experiences, and best practices.

This community should also serve as a continuous learning and professional development platform, which is asked for by migrant teachers in this study. Misinterpreted school situations or coping strategies could be discussed during such continuous learning. It could include workshops, seminars, and lectures that offer ongoing professional development opportunities that align with the transformative learning process. Teacher educators should take into account that migrant teachers are not just acquiring new knowledge and skills; they are undergoing a transformation in their professional identity, involving navigating the differences between their previous and new educational experiences. In this process, teacher educators can facilitate and assist by offering reflective and inclusive training programmes that emphasise competence development and encourage reflection on past teaching experiences and their integration or adaptation to the Swedish educational framework.

Integral to teachers' professional identity are their beliefs about teaching and learning, which involve interpreting and reinterpreting context-dependent experiences (Dos Santos, 2022; Guskey, 2002; Kalaja et al., 2016; Korthagen, 2013; Lee & Schallert, 2016; Stensmo, 1994, 2007). Pedagogical methods, which may differ from those in their home countries, can be reflected upon; however, it is equally important to verify and listen to the former ways of teaching and learning, asking how the Swedish teacher education can improve based on the migrant teacher's knowledge. In order to do that, teacher educators can provide reflective and inclusive training, emphasising competence development, by offering training programmes that encourage reflection on their past teaching experiences and how these can be integrated with or adapted to the Swedish system. This involves navigating the variances between previous and current educational experiences. Such training should be culturally sensitive and personalised, addressing the specific needs and experiences of migrant teachers, and may include mentorship to support competence development in supporting migrant teachers. Mentors who are teachers working at schools and preschools can be supported in competence development on how to support migrant teachers. Yip et al. (2022) show that migrant teachers' professional identity is critical in a professional transition. Further, Zhao and Ko (2018) highlight that teachers' perception of their professional identity is reflected in their ability to exert their agency through skills in workplace learning practices, including social aspects of learning situations. This aligns with Illeris's transformative, authentic learning environments (Illeris 2004, 2014b, 2015, 2017, 2018).

Thus, inclusive training should address the specific needs of migrant teachers, acknowledging the wide variance in their experiences and competencies. Additionally, pay special attention to cultural differences and how they impact teaching styles and classroom management. Thus, respect and maintain the unique cultural identities and knowledge of migrant teachers. The pedagogical approach to working with migrant teachers in Sweden should be holistic, encompassing professional and personal dimensions, and aim to create an inclusive, adaptive, and supportive educational environment.

Lastly, this present research project reveals several new aspects from migrant teachers' viewpoints. These migrant teachers, with their unique competence, can compare and contrast teaching paradigms, leading to an inevitably developing professional identity with additional skills assimilated into their previous one. They have a unique competence that is beneficial for a Swedish school environment that needs them. Furthermore, their journey exemplifies transformative learning, merging previous and present teaching methods and norms. This is sometimes not just adapting; they are transforming to different degrees. The interpretative framework migrant teachers navigate through is an ever-evolving journey and, for migrant teachers, a dual challenge of reconciling past experiences with contemporary contexts. Ongoing research into migrant teachers' experiences further illuminates their unique competencies and the transformative nature of their professional journey, emphasising the importance of inclusive pedagogy in leveraging and integrating their diverse experiences for a rich, multifaceted educational environment.

Challenging Aspects of Migrant Teachers' Experiences in Swedish Education

Cultural and Pedagogical Dissonance

Findings in the study show that migrant teachers face significant challenges in adapting to new teaching methods, roles, and cultural expectations. This adaptation can be a difficult and sensitive learning experience. Migrant teachers can struggle to adapt to Sweden's new pedagogical approaches, cultural norms, and values. These challenges stem from differences in their previous teaching experiences and the Swedish educational culture. The difficulties faced by migrant teachers in adapting to the Swedish educational culture stem from more profound issues of cultural and pedagogical dissonance. These challenges are not just about learning new methods but involve reconciling fundamental differences in educational philosophies and approaches.

Understanding the nature and extent of these discrepancies is vital for developing effective induction and training programmes. Migrant teachers expressed that they felt more secure, knowing about the Swedish regulations when attending schools and how to relate to parents and students. Swedish values were often brought up as a central topic during focus group interviews. This emotional tuning to a new professional environment was coupled with the challenge of establishing social connections. One study (Käck et al., 2018a) discovered the cultural aspects embedded in Swedish teacher education. It underscored the challenges migrant teachers face; it could be unfamiliar teaching methods, roles or the cultural expectations set for educators (Käck et al., 2018a). Focusing on migrant teachers during their placement, the significance of pre-service training from a migrant teacher perspective. Such training is instrumental in integrating experiences from their former educational systems with the one in Sweden, fostering a new teaching identity (Käck, 2018b). The journey of a migrant teacher in Swedish teacher education consists of transformation regarding their professional identity.

Learning is interpreted in different ways determined by earlier experiences (Illeris, 2014b, 2017), of which many of the findings give an example. Migrant teachers felt a need to discuss subjects, relations, laws, and ways of teaching and practising in relation to their former experiences. Their belief system influences how they view their teacher role and is an essential aspect of professional development (Guskey, 2002; Korthagen, 2013; Lee & Schallert, 2016; Yip et al., 2022), which is shaken when there is a vast difference between their former and new status. Wen et al. (2023) study highlights Western teachers' transformative experiences in China, navigating cultural differences through reflective practices and transforming their professional identities. This corresponds to Yip et al.'s (2022) findings that migrant teachers' professional identity is critical in the professional transition, and they link it to employment status, beliefs, and attitudes toward teaching.

Teachers with migrant backgrounds allow for external interaction and internal psychological elaboration, supporting their personal and professional development. This includes ordinary accommodation, which means understanding an aspect in a new way while accepting the differences, and transformative accommodation, which includes social, emotional, and cognitive dimensions (Illeris, 2014a, 2014b, 2014c, 2017). This sense of belonging is of utmost importance for migrant teachers' wellbeing (Kwee, 2020; Miller, 2019). In the present study, migrant teachers expressed challenges to gaining recognition for their professional identity as teachers. The low status of Swedish teachers was a shock. Still, they also struggled with language barriers, lacking recognition for their competence from the teacher educators or colleagues in school during in-practice. They felt that their competence was fully recognised; they were not students but competent teachers, and they wanted to be treated as such. Having been nurtured in different educational terrains, these teachers face the challenge of understanding Swedish pedagogy and reconciling their past experiences with sometimes new connections to their professional identities.

Transitioning to a student-centred learning environment and adapting to new examination methods and classroom dynamics are significant hurdles. Migrant teachers can face difficulties in adjusting their teaching approaches. The shift to student-centred learning and new assessment methods poses significant challenges. These challenges are not just logistical but involve a fundamental shift in the educational paradigm. Understanding the specific areas of difficulty and providing targeted support is crucial for facilitating a smoother transition.

When migrant teachers self-assess their digital skills, there is a wide disparity in digital competence among them, from digital illiterate to specialists. This variance was related to socio-economic conditions, technological accessibility, and societal restrictions in their home countries (Käck et al., 2019b, 2019c). This disparity highlights a broader issue of unequal access to technological resources and education in different parts of the world. Addressing these disparities requires a multifaceted approach, including targeted technological training and support (Käck et al., 2019a). Migrant teachers sought competence development related to digital competence in their new country (Cruishank, 2022; Käck et al., 2019b, 2019c). Initial unfamiliarity with digital technologies and variations in technological infrastructure can pose significant obstacles (Käck, 2019a; Käck et al., 2019b, 2019c).

Risk of Regressive Transformation and Vulnerability

If not adequately supported, the transformative learning process can become overwhelming, leading to defensive or regressive transformations instead of growth (Illeris, 2014a, 2014b). The transformation process can make migrant teachers feel vulnerable for a prolonged period (Kwee, 2020; Miller, 2019), mainly when there is a vast difference between their former and new status. Without adequate support, the transformative learning process can become a source of vulnerability and stress, potentially leading to a defensive posture that hinders positive professional development. Miller (2019) identified that migrants' sense of who they are is based on group membership, providing a sense of belonging while adopting a group's identity and conforming to their norms. Thus, migrant teachers felt they were not taken seriously, lacked opportunities and support, and had roles confined to behaviour management and classroom teaching. Further, Kwee (2020) identified the challenges migrated teachers face in Australia. Challenges to getting their qualifications accredited, discrepancies in classroom management, and experiences of racism and discrimination. That is why a support system is needed to help them in their career choices. Despite access to bridging programmes and courses on local curricula classroom dynamics, migrant teachers were often urged to adopt an Australian teaching style. This pressure contributed to dissatisfaction and disillusionment with some bridging programmes (Kwee, 2020). This vulnerability must be taken into consideration in teacher education. Miller (2018) identified that although migrant teachers play an important role in the workforce, they are just getting by and adjusting to the new educational system. However, scarce evidence suggests they are prospering or excelling. This is evident when teachers' vulnerabilities are taken into consideration. Yips (2023) discovered that migrant teachers' professional vulnerability, influenced by perceptions of their teaching ability by students, parents, and colleagues, impacted their transition. Lack of trust and support increased their vulnerability, especially when facing challenges with teaching competence, difficult students, and social isolation. The absence of a support network further heightened their vulnerability. Also, Bressler and Rotter (2017) link migrant teachers' professional identity with the expectations of policymakers and colleagues, with cultural, social, and political contexts as significant factors in identity formation.

In the present study, migrant teachers navigated this more or less familiar educational and social environment, asking for a support system together with Swedish teachers and, at the same time, trying to find a balance of who they are as teachers in a new country. Some situations were easy to become familiar with; others were more complicated. Is this a Swedish way of teaching well? Do

I want to become a more mentor-like teacher? What about group work? Is it a good way of teaching? There are a lot of intricate questions that migrant teachers formulate and reflect on. How do I teach in an environment that sometimes is not my cup of tea? Why is the teacher role so different, and how do I approach that? How can I grade when thinking and practising this are unfamiliar? Questions like this are brought up in the interviews. Lee and Schallert (2016) emphasise that teachers must identify their past, present, and future to understand teaching and themselves. The experiences of migrant teachers in the Swedish educational system are a complex blend of profound professional growth and significant challenges. Findings show that, while they contribute valuable perspectives and aid in enriching the educational milieu, they face challenging barriers in adapting to new teaching methodologies and cultural norms. These experiences underscore the need for comprehensive support and a culturally sensitive approach to facilitate their successful integration and professional development.

The experience of migrant teachers in Sweden, while rich with potential for growth and cross-cultural exchange, is simultaneously beset with challenges. These encompass adaptation difficulties, vulnerability, and disparities in professional needs, underscoring the necessity for targeted support and culturally sensitive pedagogical approaches. Thus, teacher education can be a facilitator of pedagogical cultural exchange and dialogue. The role of pedagogues in nurturing and guiding migrant teachers through their acculturation process is pivotal, enriching the overall teacher training paradigm.

2.4.4 Limitations and Future Research

A limitation is connected to the number of participants, eighteen individuals from thirteen countries, in the context of four Swedish universities in 2022. It is not possible to generalise, and this is a glimpse of what migrant teachers can experience in relation to their professional identity. Since education is situated both contextually and in time, the answers migrant teachers give reflect that. The most important thing is to continuously examine and assess their education and conduct research to better understand the transformation migrant teachers are reflecting. This will give us more answers on how to develop teacher education locally and globally in order to scaffold migrant teachers more sufficiently based on their own experiences. It would be interesting to see more research based on the Illeris identity model in teacher education in other countries with supplementary education for migrant teachers. It is also possible to use ongoing research to inform policy and practice in teacher education and further discuss the development of Swedish teacher education.

3 Teacher Educators from Other Countries

In this section, two of my colleagues in teacher training at Stockholm University will share their transformative educational journey, which has impacted their identity as teachers. Both have extensive insights into teaching and learning methodologies across diverse cultural landscapes. Their narratives contextualise the Illeris identity model, visualising that migrant educators undergo a profound re-evaluation and redefinition of their work identities as teachers. I will end this chapter by summarising their texts in relation to theories in Sections 2.1 and 2.2.

3.1 An Educator's Identity Crisis

My Background

31 August 2003 was the day I, Katie Obeid, landed in Sweden and the day a new phase of life began. Termed a 'kärleksinvandrare' or a love immigrant in local parlance, I carried with me a bachelor's degree in English literature and a nine-year tenure as a high school English teacher in the Middle East. My aspirations were anchored in a commitment to continue my teaching career in Sweden despite recognising the inevitable challenges. Transitioning to a new country entailed grappling not just with a foreign language but also integrating into a distinct culture, one highly revered in my home country. The journey appeared daunting yet promising. Being a language teacher, I understood that mastering a language transcended mere vocabulary acquisition; it entailed embracing a novel identity intertwined with a new culture, values, norms, and mentality.

My initial endeavour involved enrolling in rigorous language courses and dedicating myself to an eight-hour daily study regimen. Every uttered word became a notation, verb conjugations adorned my notebooks, and Swedish literature became my conduit to comprehending the nation's history, societal ethos, norms, lifestyles, and narratives. However, the most important thing that contributed to rapid language acquisition was an instantaneous affinity – a profound admiration for Swedish, akin to a serene and harmonious melody. I fell in love with it from the moment I heard the first sentence uttered by a woman at a shop I was at. In my ears, Swedish sounded like a serene and harmonious melody. It was love at first sentence. It was an enamoured response, fostering a relentless pursuit of fluency and proficiency.

Upon completion of language courses, I sought validation and qualification of my credentials from the Swedish Council of Higher Education. Simultaneously, I engaged with the Employment Service, yet encountered disheartening advice – restarting my university education appeared to be the only viable path. I thought

I didn't mind that; my affinity for learning propelled me through the labyrinth of educational opportunities. Navigating a spectrum of courses and universities, I embarked on a transformative journey at Stockholm University, undertaking a comprehensive five-and-a-half-year teacher re-certification programme specialising in English and Swedish as a second language.

Amidst relentless study sessions, often fatigued yet resolute, I pursued an academic degree in a language acquired merely years prior. My Master's thesis in English literature and dual teacher education courses provided invaluable insights, although the curriculum lacked tailored provisions for migrant teachers. Nevertheless, it facilitated profound introspection into entrenched Swedish social norms and institutional structures, pivotal to my integration into the Swedish educational landscape – heralding an epoch of socio-cultural adjustment and the emergence of a redefined teacher identity.

Parallel to my academic pursuits, I engaged as a substitute teacher across diverse Stockholm schools, further honing my pedagogical prowess. Graduating as a high school teacher in 2012 marked a significant milestone, but it was followed by arduous employment endeavours. Initial rejections echoed until an opportunity arose at a multicultural high school, enriching my teaching experience within socio-economically diverse classrooms. This exposure galvanised my passion for teaching, culminating in a deliberate shift towards seeking roles within multicultural educational settings.

Subsequent years witnessed my foray into adult education, fostering linguistic proficiency in Swedish and English among newly migrated adults. This endeavour resonated deeply, imbuing my professional journey with purpose. A serendipitous encounter in 2016 beckoned – an opportunity to instruct and guide newly migrated teachers and preschool educators from different countries at Stockholm University. The convergence felt predestined, leading to my ongoing tenure as a Project Manager for digitalisation and teacher educator in teacher education courses at Stockholm University.

A Journey of Introspection, Self-questioning, and Evaluation

August 2016 was the beginning of a long and profound journey, prompting a profound examination of my identity, especially in my capacity as an educator. Assuming the role of a teacher educator and course coordinator for foreign and international teachers and preschool educators within a project at Stockholm's university, my responsibilities encompass administrative duties, course evaluation, and continuous syllabus refinement across various teacher programmes. Embracing a contrastive pedagogical approach, I tried to illuminate disparities in philosophical ideologies, educational paradigms, curricular frameworks, and educational legislations between Sweden and diverse origin countries. I applied translanguaging strategies to accomplish those goals on a deeper academic level. I encouraged the exhaustive utilisation of linguistic resources to foster collective comprehension and meaning creation. I recognised the need for a deeper understanding of migrant teachers' professional identity in new educational contexts.

The project at Stockholm University was an interactive, experience-driven educational platform, championing the participants' experiential knowledge as a cornerstone for intercultural learning. Embracing a cultural contrast methodology, foreign educators were exposed to alternative perspectives, fostering critical self-reflection vis-à-vis their accustomed societal paradigms in comparison to the adopted ethos of their host country. This immersive process, however, unearthed challenges as migrant educators grappled with ideological incongruities and voiced scepticism towards adopting prevailing Swedish educational values. Consequently, a dichotomy emerged – a desire for affinity and validation when engaging with me juxtaposed against a more conciliatory stance with my ethnically Swedish colleagues.

Navigating these complexities engendered a profound re-evaluation of my own values and teacher identity. The alignment and disconnect between my cultural roots and evolving professional ethos became apparent as I found myself being scrutinised by educators with whom I shared a cultural kinship. Their dissent towards Swedish societal values – particularly pertaining to gender equality, pedagogical roles, and student autonomy – instigated impassioned dialogues and debates during my lectures. I endeavoured to bridge these divides, advocating for an integration of their entrenched values with the evolving educational landscape in Sweden. Facing this, I felt the need for interaction, mutual respect, and awareness of cultural assumptions in my teaching. I had to humbly listen and explain that coming to a new country and planning to work as a teacher for future generations was not going to be easy if they didn't go through an integration process of the teaching values and knowledge they carried with them and the new values they had to learn in Sweden. The lectures turned into debates where we would sometimes be able to reach a common agreement. I tried to focus on merging experiences between my experience as an educator and that of my migrant teacher students to create a more inclusive learning environment.

This transformative phase, spanning from 2016 to 2019, compelled a profound introspection into my identity evolution. The inquiry extended beyond merely embracing a new institutional or discourse-driven identity – it delved into the quest for a nuanced global or transnational teacher identity. My trajectory in Sweden, navigating linguistic acquisition and transitioning from a language instructor to an educator, fostered a multifaceted identity encompassing roles as a perpetual learner, critical thinker, and global citizen. Nonetheless, this process remains an ongoing, adaptive evolution; necessitating continued translanguaging, transcultural acumen, and transnational fluency – integral attributes accrued through immersive socialisation and critical intellectual engagement (Gao, 2021).

3.2 My Educational Journey

Introduction

Originally from Middle East, I, Manal Musa, moved to Sweden in 2002. In my former country, I earned a Master's Degree in Pedagogy and taught at a high school for seven years. After studying Swedish for educators in Sweden, I joined the 'Further Education for Foreign Teachers' programme in 2007 and received my Swedish teacher certification in 2009. I later attained a Master's in Educational Leadership from Uppsala University. Additionally, I have a degree from Stockholm University's National School Leadership Training Programme. Before my current role as a project manager, teacher educator and assistant director of studies at Stockholm University, I worked as a teacher and educational leader in Sweden for a decade, helping educators improve their ICT skills.

After moving from my former country and residing in Sweden for over two decades, I possess a comprehensive and multicultural network. This network offers daily challenges that foster my personal growth. This network's diverse relationships and experiences allow me to view the world with an open mind. Through family, friends, and colleagues, along with a long education journey and countless study hours, I have gained the vital tools and resources needed to perform in this line of work.

Development as an Educator

I have thought about these aspects over the years and have encountered and worked continuously to deliver on the expectations placed on me as an educator. I felt the need to understand everything happening within Swedish teacher education and the Swedish school system. I pondered how to approach my thinking now in relation to my previous teacher training and what I had learned through Swedish teacher education. A key consideration for me was how to strike a balance between these experiences to shape my pedagogical leadership. It concerns my leadership and role as a teacher, in which norms dominate the learning environment and how I support my students best, regardless of their circumstances.

An example of an expectation that has changed and influenced my way of working over time and place is that of the goal. There is a big difference between working results-orientedly because what was expected was passing the exam/course and getting a good grade rather than working for lifelong learning, where one learns to develop, not for exam opportunities. Another example is expectations. My students expected to get knowledge from me as the lecturer, which affected their efforts. Most of them were passive; there was no group work then, and the entire lesson was mostly my lecture and possibly testing their knowledge through questions and examinations.

A concrete example illustrating the different cultural expectations of teachers is in a seminar with my Swedish teacher colleague; we shared teaching responsibilities for foreign teacher students. Despite clear instructions and a timetable, after a coffee break, the students chatted instead of continuing to work in groups and starting the task. My colleague was surprised, and I explained that foreign teacher students expected a direct signal to begin. She did so, and they started immediately. This sparked a discussion on the expectations placed on teachers. This example highlights the importance of understanding and adapting to different cultural and pedagogical expectations among students (Dervin, 2023). Teachers must be aware that different students may have various expectations regarding how the teaching and work should be structured and communicated, even small things. Being attentive to these expectations can create a more inclusive and successful learning environment for all students.

I have revised my understanding and approach during my personal development and with the addition of new work experiences. In this process, I have sometimes merged my new experiences with the old ones, contributing to a more comprehensive view of my work and professional development. I developed my interpretation of my leadership as a teacher, which is about being a facilitator and coaching my students throughout the process rather than taking over the entire learning situation, supporting them to reassess and restructure their thoughts, values, and perspectives. A significant change in my approach has also involved creating a supportive, collaborative environment within groups and identifying different strategies for each student's learning. I have continuously evaluated and adjusted my approach both during and after the learning process to ensure ongoing progress. This contrasts with my previous experiences, where a lack of self-reflection and more focus on students' outcomes and performance were more prominent than the teacher's methodology. The educator's proficiency in interaction, communication, and motivation will influence how they act in different situations and how effectively knowledge transfer and learning occur in the classroom. Therefore, developing and enhancing these skills is crucial to creating a stimulating and successful learning environment for students.

With my background and broad experiences, I have the tools and resources to contribute to this line of work; nonetheless, this becomes true in getting students to commit to learning, taking their part in the learning process and challenging them forward. I have developed in my professional role when it comes to interactive teaching by being creative in how interaction can be done and how to get students to participate in their own education. My view on student participation has evolved as an educator, especially during my professional work in Sweden. The way I perceive participation and interaction has primarily affected the understanding and interpretation of the concepts of inclusion and participation, as well as the level of engagement, all of which can vary depending on the individual student.

Working with Student Teachers from Other Countries

To promote effective learning, it is necessary to recognise and support students' and learners' experiences and linguistic competencies. This may involve providing resources, tools, and education that encourage positive interaction (Cenoz & Gorter, 2022). As an educator, I created a more inclusive learning environment by enhancing access to knowledge and promoting experience and linguistic competencies among my students.

Many methods are available to ensure that qualitative learning takes place, but all of them focus on the individual who is there to learn. In my work with a heterogeneous group of students with different skills, abilities, and cultural backgrounds, great demands are placed on me to inspire and engage each one, regardless of their experiences, backgrounds, and opinions. My view on learning and teaching differs from that of the students aspiring to become teachers themselves, and the one thing that I always need to deliver upon is to ensure that I am carrying out my duties in a professional manner. Working with students aspiring to become teachers/educators from other countries really highlights the importance of the socio-cultural perspective on learning. Through communication and interaction with my students, we create a meaningful context for learning. Embracing the socio-cultural perspective, which makes it easier to understand and inherit knowledge, is something I notice my students do. Through their in-service training, they have been able to communicate and engage, as well as teach in various ways and possess the ability to use different teaching strategies. However, language barriers have become a struggle for some students, as they sometimes find it hard to engage in dialogue. In this context, language is important as it transfers perceptions and expresses them in speech or writing. For this reason, to be able to provide educational learning and stay up-to-date, the teacher must enter a lifelong learning state of mind. Furthermore, general education today must also offer lifelong learning; the increased accessibility to ICT has changed the conditions for learning. In my work, I use digital tools and social media to promote learning in the desired direction. However, what the students learn depends on many different factors, including their background, knowledge, abilities, and needs, which differ enormously.

Information and communication technology is another challenge that some of my students have struggled with, but I feel that several of them have been able to handle and master it over time during the course. In order to succeed, I also need to be flexible in my methods, which means they change depending on the unique teaching situation, for me to succeed. Group work is instructive but, in some cases, has been a challenge due to socio-cultural differences and values. This demands me as a teacher to create conditions for achieving better cooperation between all students regardless of background or experience.

Insights That I Can Bring to Teacher Training

My work goal is always to create a creative pedagogical process for my students, which results in the students also wanting to take responsibility for their further development. In my teaching and educational process, I make sure that the knowledge and educational objectives are clear and understood by my students. As an educator, I must always anchor a goal with the students. This is done by clarifying how I view the goal in question and then clarifying how the students view the goal. I must be clear about the expectations, and it is equally important that the student is involved in that set of expectations. It could be about encouraging a dialogue regarding the teacher's role and powers in their country of education versus in Sweden. We then begin to analyse and reflect on the similarities and differences between their country of education and Sweden until we create an overall picture of the role and powers of the teacher in Sweden. In my teaching, I also use current pedagogical teaching methods that give me a better insight into students' learning processes. I also use different forms of assessments, and I dare to try new ones as well. Assessment generally takes place at the end of the course (summative assessment), which can be called an assessment of learning. However, as an educator, I also see the importance of carrying out formative assessments, where much light is put on constructive dialogues and feedback to support my students during the whole learning process (Golding & Adam, 2016).

In conclusion, it is my belief that the future will be more about lifelong learning, where it is up to the individual to ensure their own development.

That is, to plant a seed on how important it is to stay up-to-date and create a desire within every student to develop oneself (Graham et al., 2015). Finally, as a committed educator, I want to improve my professional role, as this is a very important part of my professional identity. I love what I do, as I can create learning possibilities daily by elaborating and testing new ideas and best practices to help others grow. This desire and creativity contribute to developing the university's learning environment.

3.3 Summary

Both Katie Obeid and Manal Musa moved from their home countries in the Middle East to Sweden, undergoing cultural and professional transitions. Their narratives highlight the challenges and learning experiences associated with adapting to a new cultural and educational environment. Each educator underwent a process of professional re-certification in Sweden. This journey involved acquiring new linguistic skills and adapting to the Swedish educational system's methodologies and ideologies. Both texts underscore the importance of language in influencing their professional identities. Learning Swedish was more than just acquiring a new language; it was integral to their integration into the Swedish culture and educational system. Obeid and Musa both came from traditional teaching roles and changed them to more facilitative and student-centred approaches, reflecting a shift in their work identities and teaching methodologies. Their experiences and competence in teaching and interacting with students and educators from various cultural backgrounds highlight their adaptability and the importance of understanding diverse educational needs and expectations.

Katie Obeid shares her odyssey as a migrant teacher from native in a country in the Middle East to unfamiliar Sweden, giving us examples of identity reflections and transformative learning (Illeris, 2014a, 2015; Taylor, 2009) in her professional landscape. Some of her transitions relate to part-identities (Illeris, 2014a), mastering a new language, understanding Swedish culture's subtleties, and grasping cultural shifts, perspectives, and values. Furthermore, as a teacher, new methods in the Swedish educational system presented additional layers. Obeid highlights the multifaceted nature of transitioning to an unfamiliar teaching and learning environment with new ways of thinking and practising (Käck, 2019; Kreber, 2009). She competently aligns her teaching approach to address students' diverse cultural backgrounds. Obeid expressed that competence development is central for her, bringing many qualifications from the Middle East. However, she cultivated a set of competencies tailored to her new context to thrive in a new environment. Thus, she shows that competencies are qualifications and the ability to function in new situations (Illeris, 2014a, 2014b, 2014c, 2015).

Embedded within Obeid's transformative journey are Taylor's core elements for transformative practice (2009). Her move from the Middle East to Sweden, with its manifold challenges, gave her profound personal and professional experiences and room for critical reflection with the results of a changing teaching identity and, thus, work identity. Even though it was sometimes challenging, engaging dialogues and discussions, especially with other newly migrated teachers, enriched her perspectives and pedagogical approach. Sometimes, the discussions with migrant teachers were challenging concerning fundamental values in Swedish laws, curricula and ordinances that determine the value base in Sweden (The National Agency for Education, 2013; 2019; 2022; Ministry of Education and Research, 2011, 2014a), a value base researched by Puranen (2019).

Both Obeid's experiences and Illeris' theoretical framework stress that transformative learning is not just cognitive but also involves emotional and social dimensions. Transformation is not linear, and this reminds us of all migrant teachers' challenges in their transformative journeys and all teachers worldwide. Transformative learning considers all human beings (Illeris, 2014b, 2017) in a liquid society (Bauman, 2000). In 'An Educator's Identity Crisis', Obeid's narrative vividly illustrates the concepts discussed in Illeris' works on transformative learning and identity. Her experiences as a migrant educator in Sweden embody the multifaceted nature of transformative learning, where language, culture, work identity, and pedagogical approaches are deeply interwoven. This underscores Illeris' theoretical framework and the relevance of his redefinition of transformative learning through the lens of identity layers. Obeid's narrative is intricately woven within dimensions of her identity – as a learner, educator, migrant, and global citizen (Illeris, 2014b) – and provides a vivid tableau of the challenges, triumphs, and transformative moments that define the journey of integrating into new educational and cultural horizons. Obeid expresses that she fostered a multifaceted identity encompassing roles as a critical thinker and global citizen. This is in line with Dos Santos (2022) research among English teachers in South Korea, where the international experiences upgraded their teaching skills and sense of internationalisation.

Manal Musa's central theme concerns her identity, experiences, and insights as an educator. Distinguished by a rich educational background, the author has navigated two distinct educational paradigms, visible in her adaptability and understanding of cultural and pedagogical differences. Acknowledging and adapting to different cultural expectations in the classroom demonstrates an understanding of the interplay between societal dynamics and individual teaching approaches. Musa positions herself as a facilitator, advocating for a collaborative teaching approach. This is complemented by lifelong learning, emphasising its significance for academic growth and holistic personal and professional development. Musa describes her transition from a lecture-driven methodology to an interactive, student-centred approach as part of her transformative learning and teaching experience (Illeris, 2014a, 2014b, 2017). Furthermore, her teachers' beliefs involve creating a nurturing, adaptable environment, prioritising understanding students' cultural and individual backgrounds.

Musa gives an example of unfamiliar ways of thinking and practising migrant teachers can experience in Swedish teacher education (Käck et al., 2018a). This example of a seminar with migrant teachers illustrates both the preference layer and personality layer in the Illeris identity model (Illeris, 2014a, 2014b, 2017) as well as unfamiliar ways of thinking and practising (Kreber, 2009). The teacher educator wonders why they do not work, and the migrant teachers think it is strange that the teacher educator does not act as they are used to. This is culturally embedded in teacher education, and it is not about lazy students or bad teachers. It is about clear communication in a diverse setting. It could be seen as something unimportant one has to adjust (preference layer). At a personality level, it concerns communication habits, collaboration (Illeris, 2014b, 2017), and the relationship between the teacher educator and migrant teachers. The educator's experiences in navigating cultural and pedagogical differences align with Illeris' insights into the complexities of identity in transformative learning, especially in multicultural educational environments. Further, her commitment to lifelong learning and adapting to new educational technologies and methods resonates with the idea of continuous identity and professional development. The narrative provides a practical illustration of Illeris' theoretical framework (Illeris, 2014a, 2014b, 2017), emphasising the significance of identity transformation in the context of cultural transitions, pedagogical adaptation, and professional development. The educator's experiences embody the multifaceted nature of transformative learning, where cultural, professional, and pedagogical aspects are deeply interwoven. This analysis underlines the relevance and depth of Illeris' redefinition of transformative learning through the lens of identity, particularly in understanding the complexities of identity evolution in cross-cultural educational contexts.

Both Obeid's and Musa's narratives offer insights into the experiences of educators who navigate transformative learning and identity changes in a cross-cultural context. There are transformative aspects of learning where moving between cultures significantly impacts one's identity, personally and professionally. While they share common themes such as cultural transition, language learning, and pedagogical adaptation, their journeys highlight unique challenges and personal growth trajectories. Their stories enrich our understanding of the multifaceted nature of transformative learning and are redefined in diverse educational settings.

4 Conclusion and Future Directions

We can enhance the migrant teachers' educational experience when they attend teacher education in different countries. In this section, I will give some examples. First, I will discuss migrant-centred teacher education, then share a model as an example of incorporating redefined transformative learning in programmes and courses.

4.1 Migrant-Centred Teacher Education

This Element aims to gain deeper insight into the redefinition of migrant teachers' professional identity when they experience a new educational context. Thus, it is important to remember that migrant teachers are a heterogeneous group with a wide range of familiar to unfamiliar ways of thinking and practising (Entwistle, 2003; Kreber, 2009). According to Yip (2023), teacher mobility has become a global phenomenon that impacts education worldwide.

Teachers express identity as an important component to negotiate when moving to another country, which makes redefining transformative learning suitable as it targets changes in the learners' identity (Illeris, 2014a, 2014b, 2014c). Who am I as a teacher in a new country? Internationally, teachers ask themselves and negotiate as an essential component. In order to understand oneself as a teacher, one has to identify and coordinate one's past, present, and future, which makes migrant teachers talk about a transformed professional identity with additional skills. When migrant teachers move to Sweden, they experience an unknown environment. This is a challenge that has become more common in modern higher education. Ryan and Carroll (2005) mention how academic and cultural shocks can make even the most successful students lose their knowledge of learning practices. Dos Santos (2022) also points out the culture shock teachers can experience, in this case, English teachers in South Korea. However, Norberg (2000) states that a monocultural approach is common in teacher education. This generalisation and homogenisation are problematic, which is evident when a teacher or student teacher is required to teach in a diverse classroom. There are risks associated with highlighting differences and making diversity invisible. However, one path forward may be interaction. According to Sjögren (2005), there are three dimensions of teaching in an intercultural setting: (a) approaches with mutual respect, reflexivity and critical thinking, (b) intercultural content knowledge which pervades education and (c) customised working methods.

In research, there are mixed opinions on whether special support is necessary for international students. Even though monocultural teaching is common, homogenisation in teaching is problematic when education is culturally diverse. Cultural bias has been discovered in examinations and coursework assignments, penalising international students in ways that exceed differences in ability levels (De Vita, 2002). Therefore, Moloney and Saltmarsh (2016) argue that teacher education must be better at considering students' diversity, as this is something that schools naturally expect from teachers. Additionally, teacher educators should acquire knowledge about the student teacher's previous cultural context to enhance their learning potential, which migrant teachers express is lacking today (Käck, 2019a). Various cultural assumptions about power relations, such as the ones between teacher and student and how teaching is managed, should become more apparent for teacher educators and student teachers (Nguyen et al., 2006). Previous research is primarily centred around teacher mobility and the encounter, transition, and adjustment to unfamiliar educational contexts (Bense, 2016; Collins & Reid, 2012; Cross et al., 2011; Donlevy et al., 2016; Miller, 2018; Proyer et al., 2019). Thus, identity and transformative learning can be a good support in designing migrant teacher-centred learning (Käck, 2019a). Migrant teachers that enter the Australian educational system have a scarcity of culturally specific knowledge regarding education. However, there are aids to help the teachers develop their professional identity, such as a mentoring relationship (Cruickshank, 2022; Peeler & Jane, 2005; Yan, 2021). Teachers' belief systems lie at the core of their professional identity. According to Yip et al. (2022), the professional identity of migrant teachers plays a crucial role during their professional transition, influencing their employment status, beliefs, and attitudes towards teaching. Further, Yips' (2023) critical finding is that professional vulnerability is an essential emotion affecting the teachers' professional transition, impacted by their perceived teaching competence by students, parents, and colleagues. There was a shift in migrant teachers' professional identity concerning their beliefs and skills as part of their new educational context.

In migrant-centred teacher education, it's vital to consider this when designing courses, bridging programmes, or initiatives for authentic competence development. Bressler and Rotter (2017) argue that the professional identity of migrant teachers aligns with the expectations set by policymakers and peers. Therefore, considering the cultural, social, and political contexts becomes essential in identity formation – something consistently expressed by migrant teachers in my research and teaching experiences. Regrettably, Miller (2018, 2019) found compelling evidence that migrant teachers merely cope within the new educational system rather than thriving due to a lack of support. By actively listening to their needs, we can significantly enhance our support for this crucial workforce, especially given today's multicultural context.

While there are significant positive implications in terms of professional growth, cultural enrichment, and collaborative learning, there are also notable challenges related to adaptation, vulnerability, and disparities in needs and competencies. This can be dealt with when inclusively working with teacher education. The next part will give a model of how to be sensitive and inclusive, not monocultural, when designing teaching and learning in teacher education.

4.2 Process Model in Teacher Education

This is a process model of teaching presented here with some examples. The redefined transformative theory, which targets changes in the learner's identity, is used to develop this model (Käck, 2019a). Migrant teachers are trained teachers and student teachers at the same time. As student teachers, they learn about ways of thinking and practising designed for Swedish teacher education. Their previous experiences, understanding of learning, and how they viewed their previous learning context influence how they experience and approach the new learning environment. Moreover, using this concept in a methodical and theoretical framework makes it possible to recognise what a specific group of students in a particular learning and teaching environment do not know. Additionally, this can aid teachers in suitably adapting their teaching. In Sweden, teacher educators are also impacted by their own ways of thinking and practising. It influences how and in what ways they expect teachers with migrant backgrounds to learn. For example, it impacts how they present the course material and how they create the teaching and learning environment. These ways of thinking and practising transcend disciplinary boundaries and are cognitive, social, and performative. The participants acknowledged unfamiliarity at several levels, including (a) the individual level, including individual sides of professional identity; (b) the group level, for instance, group work among teachers or learning in social environments; and (c) society, which means to recognise their teacher role in a broader perspective.

This process model was developed in relation to findings and theories that I (Käck, 2019a, 2022) have worked on both as a researcher and educational developer in higher education (see Figure 2). This can aid teacher educators in changing monocultural teaching to an inclusive practice, integrating diversity. The following steps in Figure 2 are further explained.

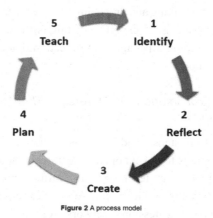

Figure 2 A process model

Figure 2 A process model

Step 1: Identify Unfamiliar Ways of Thinking and Practising

The first step is to identify and recognise unique traditions and practices, the ways of thinking and practising that influence teaching strategy and activities in ongoing teaching and learning. These are often tacit knowledge within a discipline, department, or culture (Entwistle, 2003; Kreber, 2009). What do migrant teachers express in relation to experiences, sometimes experienced as unfamiliar, in a new educational context? The unfamiliar ways of thinking and practising can relate to and describe various individual, group, or institutional levels. Using quantitative and qualitative methods makes gaining more knowledge as a teacher educator possible. It can be course evaluations, surveys, oral evaluations, and discussions. Some subjects can be sensitive, and giving some anonymity can be helpful. However, interviews give more in-depth knowledge.

Step 2: Reflect on Current Ways of Thinking and Practising (in courses, programmes, and departments)

When the unfamiliarity is identified, it is beneficial to self-reflect on the current education with its ways of thinking and practising to learn from it and develop and improve the quality of teacher education. Migrant teachers are a great asset with amazing competence. Listening to educated teachers from other countries gives rare insights into how to develop courses and programmes further. The relevant question is whether the current way of teaching and learning is based on research and experience. Why is your education designed a certain way, and what are the results? Can newer research shed light on teaching and learning?

Are there other ways of thinking and practising that are more suitable? What can be learned from the pedagogical expertise of migrant teachers from different parts of the world? Keeping a pedagogical reflection diary and writing down your insights can be good.

Step 3: Create Practical Solutions and Strategies That Make Current Ways of Thinking and Practising More Transparent for the Students

With the knowledge from steps 1 and 2, now is the time to create solutions and strategies. One example is to design open educational resources that make the ways of thinking, practising, teaching, and learning more transparent for migrant teachers. Can you record lecturers? Another example is to start mentoring programmes and build professional networks for them where they can meet and discuss their new educational context. If the digital teaching and learning environment is unfamiliar, there is a need to discuss both digital technologies and unfamiliar teaching and learning strategies.

Step 4: Plan for Authentic Competence Development and Transformative Learning

When planning for transformative learning and authentic competence development, it is good to have strategies for a change- and learner-centred, problem-oriented teaching and learning approach related to practice (Owens, 2018; Taylor, 2009). This includes individual experiences and critical reflections in dialogue with others. Transformative learning is grounded in a holistic orientation that includes cognitive, emotional, and social aspects. Furthermore, authentic competence development requires (a) engagement, (b) practice/problem, and (c) reflection (Illeris, 2014b, 2017). In order to plan for transformative learning and authentic competence development, teacher educators need to know the supplementary programme and the migrant teachers' backgrounds. This will help migrant teachers process their professional background and identity in relation to new ways of thinking and practising. In this process, it is important not to talk about migrant teachers but to ask them directly what they need. What questions do they have?

Step 5: New Teaching and Learning Strategies Suitable for the Targeted Student Cohort

With the knowledge from steps 1–4, the teacher educators know more about what the migrant teachers experience as unfamiliar and have new strategies and plans to meet their needs. It is time to teach with the new strategies and content identified in steps 1–4. There are a few examples: when discussing course literature – include questions that make migrant teachers reflect on the literature in relation to their prior knowledge and how they will use the content in their practice; oral examinations where they reflect on their professional identity; and practice or case-based assignments.

Steps 1 to 5 All Over Again Regularly

The process is cyclic, and the work to assess and identify continues since this student group, society and education change constantly. That is why steps 1 to 5 should be repeated regularly.

4.3 Future Directions

Ideally, monocultural teaching should be exchanged for a more inclusive way of teaching and learning (Bodström et al., 2020; Frantik et al., 2021; Kansteiner et al., 2021; Proyer et al., 2019; Terhart et al., 2020; Wen et al., 2023). Investigating migrant teachers can lead to a deeper understanding of how competence is approached in Swedish teacher education and what can be done additionally to aid them in their education and work as student teachers. This research can help improve examinations and assessments, making education more equal and inclusive. The goal is for teacher educators and migrant teachers to merge their different experiences to develop a more inclusive learning environment for everyone. This also further helps evolve digital competence in Swedish teacher education (Käck, 2012). The goal of transformative learning is to make authentic competence development more diverse. When working together globally, digital technologies are carriers which allow for a more inclusive educator programme across nations (Wen et al., 2023). Collaboration is one way to increase educators' intercultural relationships (Proyer et al., 2019; Wen, 2023). I worked on a project called Requalification of (recently) immigrated and refugee teachers in Europe – R/EQUAL, a collaboration between teacher educations at four European universities: The University of Cologne Mercator Institute for Literacy and Language Education, the University of Vienna, Stockholm University, and the University of Education Weingarten. The project's aim focused on international networking, cooperation, and material for higher education. Thus, results were spread on planning and implementing programmes for (recently) immigrant refugee teachers. All results are available in English, German, and Swedish and can be seen at the following website: https://blog.hf.uni- koeln.de/immigrated-and-refu gee-teachers-requal/. In the results, participants discussed, for example, obstacles to entering the teaching profession and experiences of working as a teacher in Germany, Austria, and Sweden (Bodström et al., 2020; Frantik et al., 2021; Kansteiner et al., 2021; Proyer et al., 2019; Terhart et al., 2020). All references can be found in German, Swedish, and English at: https://blog.hf.uni- koeln.de/ immigrated-and-refugee-teachers-requal/.

Further collaboration and research in teacher education worldwide could enhance our knowledge and education at the same time. This can inform policy and practice to ensure relevant support. Some pedagogical implications for the future could be recognising comprehensive education and developing induction programmes that address the cognitive, social, and emotional aspects of trans-formation for migrant teachers. These programmes should include pedagogical, cultural orientation, peer support networks, and professional development opportunities. It is important to facilitate dialogue and exchange between Swedish and migrant educators, which fosters mutual understanding and a more inclusive educational environment.

In conclusion, the experiences of migrant teachers in the Swedish educational system present a complex interplay of professional growth and significant challenges. A nuanced understanding of these experiences is essential for developing targeted supplementary education. By addressing these challenges and harnessing the positive aspects of their experiences, the Swedish educa-tional system can move towards a more inclusive, diverse, and dynamic future. This Element concerns migrant teachers' transformation, how they redefine their professional identity, and how this can be supported in teacher education. By reflecting on how migrant-centred learning can be achieved, even if just a few in a group, and designing the teaching and learning environment with this as a starting point, there will be many more learning experiences for the whole group and the teacher educators.

References

Asmus, B. M. (2015). *Literacy practices among migrant teachers: Educator perspectives and critical observations.* Diss. 732. Western Michigan University. https://scholarworks.wmich.edu/dis-sertations/732.

Baldwin, C. K. & Motter, A. E. (2021). Autoethnographic dance and transformative learning: Exploring self-reflexive identity work and change., *Journal of Transformative Education*, 19(2), pp. 107–126. https://doi.org/10.1177/154134 4620943681.

Bauman, Z. (2000). *Liquid modernity.* Cambridge: Polity Press.

Bautista, A. & Ortega-Ruiz, R. (2015). Teacher professional development: International perspectives and approaches. *Psychology, Society and Education*, 7(3), pp. 343–355. https://doi.org/10.25115/psye.v7i3.1020.

Bennett, M. J. (2012, February 15). Turning cross-cultural contact into intercultural learning. Paper presented at the *8th International Congress on Higher Education*, Havana: Cuba.

Bense, K. (2016). International teacher mobility and migration: A review and synthesis of the current empirical research and literature. *Educational Research Review*, 17, pp. 37–49.

Bodström, H., Käck, A., Linné, T. et al. (2020). *IO2 – Teaching and Learning in Multilingual Contexts in Programmes for Internationally Trained Teachers in Europe.* https://blog.hf.uni-koeln.de/immigrated-and-refugee-teachers-requal/manual/.

Bressler, C. & Rotter, C. (2017). The relevance of a migration background to the professional identity of teachers. *International Journal of Higher Education*, 6(1), pp. 239–250.

Byram, M. (1997). *Teaching and assessing intercultural communicative competence.* Clevedon, UK: Multilingual Matters.

Bryman, A. (2012). *Social Research Methods.* 4th ed., Oxford: Oxford University Press.

Carretero, S., Vuorikari, R. & Punie, Y. (2017). DigComp 2.1: The digital competence framework for citizens with eight proficiency levels and examples of use. https://doi.org/10.2760/38842.

Cenoz, J. & Gorter, D. (2022). Pedagogical translanguaging and its application to language classes. *RELC Journal: A Journal of Language Teaching and Research*, 53(2), pp. 342–354. doi: 10.1177/00336882221082751.

Chamberlin-Quinlisk, C. (2013). Media, technology, and intercultural education. *Intercultural Education*, 24, pp. 297–302. https://doi.org/10.1080/14675986.2013.813656.

Collins, J. & Reid, C. (2012). Immigrant teachers in Australia. *Cosmopolitan Civil Societies: An Interdisciplinary Journal*, 4(2), pp. 38–61.

Cornelius, Å. & Bredänge, G. (eds.) (2011). All världens lärare i Sverige: utländska lärares vidareutbildning. [All the world's teachers in Sweden: foreign teachers' further education]. Stockholms universitet.

Council of Europe. (1997). Convention on the Recognition of Qualifications concerning Higher Education in the European Region. www.coe.int/en/web/conventions/full-list/-/conventions/treaty/165[2019-07-07].

Council of Europe. (2010). Revised Recommendation on Criteria and Procedures for the Assessment of Foreign Qualifications. Adopted by the Lisbon Recognition Convention Committee at its fifth meeting, Sèvres. www.coe.int/t/dg4/high-ereducation/Recognition/Criteria%20and%20proce-dures_EN.asp#TopOfPage[2019-07-07]

Cousin, G. (2009). Researching Learning in Higher Education: An introduction to contemporary methods and approaches. New York: Routledge. https://doi.org/10.4324/9780203884584.

Creswell, J. W., & Plano Clark, V. L. (2017). *Designing and Conducting Mixed Methods Research*. 3rd ed., Los Angeles, CA: SAGE.

Creswell, J. W., & Plano Clark, V. L. (2011). *Designing and conducting mixed methods research*. 2nd ed., Los Angeles, CA: SAGE. https://doi.org/978-1-4129-7517-9.

Cross, D. I., Hong, J., & Williams-Johnson, M. (2011). It's not better or worse, it's just different: Examining Jamaican teachers' pedagogical and emotional experiences. *Teacher Development*, 15(4), pp. 499–515.

Cruickshank, K. (2022). Creating pathways for internationally educated teachers into the teaching profession: Practices, policies and problems in the Australian context. *European Educational Research Journal*, 21(2), pp. 230–246. https://doi.org/10.1177/14749041211048983.

Dervin, F. (2023). *Interculturality, Criticality and Reflexivity in Teacher Education*. Cambridge: Cambridge University Press.

De Vita, G. (2002). Cultural equivalence in the assessment of home and international business management students: A UK exploratory study. *Studies in Higher Education*, 27(2), pp. 221–231.

Donlevy, V., Mejerkord, A., & Rajania, A. (2016). Study on the diversity within the teaching profession with particular focus on migrant and minority background. Annexes to the Final Report to DG Education and Culture of the European Commission.

Dos Santos, L. M. (2022). Can I teach abroad? Motivations and decision-making processes of teachers to the international locations. *Journal of Curriculum and Teaching*, 11(4), pp. 13–23. https://doi.org/10.5430/jct.v11n4p13.

Eatwell, J., Milgate, M., & Newman, P. (eds.) (1998). *The New Palgrave Dictionary of Economics*. London: Macmillan.

Eckerdal, A. (2009). Ways of Thinking and Practising in Introductory Programming. Technical Report 2009-002. Uppsala University. www.it.uu.se/research/publications/reports/2009-002/2009-002-nc.pdf.

Edwards, D. H. (2014). *Migrant Teachers: A Case Study*. Diss. University of Maryland. https://doi.org/10.13016/M2X603

Enochsson, A-B. (2009). ICT in Initial Teacher Training – Sweden country report. OECD.

Ennerberg, E., & Economou, C. (2022). Career adaptability among migrant teachers re-entering the labour market: A life course perspective. *Vocations and Learning*, 15(2), pp. 341–357. https://doi.org/10.1007/s12186-022-09290-y.

Ennser-Kananen, J., & Ruohotie-Lyhty, M. (2023). 'I'm a foreign teacher': Legitimate positionings in the stories of a migrant teacher. *Journal of Education for Teaching*, 49(3), pp.1–16.

Entwistle, N. (2003). Concepts and conceptual frameworks underpinning the ETL project. *Occasional Report*, 3, pp. 3–4.

Entwistle, N., McCune, V., & Hounsell, J. (2002). Approaches to Studying and Perceptions of University Teaching-Learning Environments: Concepts, Measures and Preliminary Findings. ETL Project Report 1. Universities of Edinburgh, Coventry and Durham.

Ertmer, P. A. (2005). Teacher pedagogical beliefs: The final frontier in our quest for technology integration? *Educational Technology Research and Development*, 53(4), pp. 25–39.

Ertmer, P. A., & Ottenbreit-Leftwich, A. (2010). Teacher technology change: How knowledge, confidence, beliefs, and culture intersect. *Journal of Research on Technology in Education*, 42(3), pp. 255–284. https://doi.org/10.1080/15391523.2010.10782551.

Eslamdoost, S., King, K. A., & Tajeddin, Z. (2020). Professional identity conflict and (re)construction among English teachers in Iran. *Journal of Language, Identity & Education*, 19(5), pp. 327–341. https://doi.org/10.1080/15348458.2019.1676157.

Frantik, P., Terhart, H., Kansteiner, K. et al. (2021). IO5 – Evaluation Report of the Participatory Approach in R/EQUAL and the Partner Programmes. https://blog.hf.uni-koeln.de/immigrated-and-refugee-teachers-requal/evaluation/.

Gao, Y. (2021). How do language learning, teaching, and transnational experiences (re)shape an EFLer's identities? A critical ethnographic narrative. *SAGE Open*, 11(3). https://doi.org/10.1177/21582440211031211.

Golding, C., & Adam, L. (2016). Evaluate to improve: Useful approaches to student evaluation. *Assessment & Evaluation in Higher Education*, 41(1), pp. 1–14. http://dx.doi.org/10.1080/02602938.2014.976810.

Golding, C., & Adam, C. (2016). *Teacher Education and Lifelong Learning*. London: Routledge.

Graham, L., Misfeldt, M., Rautiainen, M., & Debauche, A. (2015). Teachers learning for life: Professional development and teacher learning in Finland, Sweden and Denmark. *Policy and Practice in Education*, 27.

Graham, L., Berman, J., & Bellert, A. (2015). *Sustainable Learning: Inclusive Practices for 21st-Century Classrooms*. Cambridge: Cambridge University Press. doi:10.1017/CBO9781107280243.

Guskey, T. R. (2002). Professional development and teacher change. *Teachers and Teaching*, 8(3), pp. 381–391. https://doi.org/10.1080/135406002100000512.

Hannon, J., & D'Netto, B. (2007). Cultural diversity online: Student engagement with learning technologies. *International Journal of Educational Management*, 21(5), pp. 418–432. https://doi.org/10.1108/09513540710760192.

Hermerén, G. (2017). *Good Research Practice*. Stockholm: The Swedish Research Council.

Hounsell, D., & Anderson, C. (2009). Ways of thinking and practicing in biology and history: Disciplinary aspects of teaching and learning environments. In C. Kreber (ed.), *The University and Its Disciplines: Teaching and Learning within and beyond Disciplinary Boundaries*. New York: Routledge.

Illeris, K. (2018). An overview of the history of learning theory. *European Journal of Education*, 53(1), pp. 86–101. https://doi.org/10.1111/ejed.12265.

Illeris, K. (2017). *Learning, Development and Education: From Learning Theory to Education and Practice*. London: Routledge.

Illeris, K. (2015). Transformative learning in higher education. *Journal of Transformative Learning*, 3(1), pp. 46–51.

Illeris, K. (2014a). Transformative learning and identity. *Journal of Transformative Education*, 12(2), pp. 148–163. https://doi.org/10.1177/1541344614548423.

Illeris, K. (2014b). *Transformative Learning and Identity*. London: Routledge. https://doi.org/10.4324/9780203795286.

Illeris, K. (2014c). Transformative learning redefined: As changes in elements of the identity. *International Journal of Lifelong Education*, 33(5), pp. 573–586. https://doi.org/10.1080/02601370.2014.917128.

Illeris, K. (2011). *The SAGE Handbook of Workplace Learning*. London: SAGE. https://doi.org/10.4135/9781446200940.

Illeris, K. (2004). Transformative learning in the perspective of a comprehensive learning theory. *Journal of Transformative Education*, 2(2), pp. 79–89. https://doi.org/10.1177/1541344603262315.

Citation when re-printing the map: The Inglehart-Welzel World Cultural Map – World Values Survey 7 (2023). www.worldvaluessurvey.org/2024-02-02.

Kalaja, P., Barcelos, A. M. F., Aro, M. & Ruohotie-Lyhty, M. (2016). *Beliefs, Agency and Identity in Foreign Language Learning and Teaching*. Basingstoke, UK: Palgrave Macmillan.

Kansteiner, K., Schneider, A., Terhart, H. et al. (2021). Teacher Education and (Re-)Qualification in the Context of Teacher Migration. An Interview Study on Experiences and Expectations in four European Programmes for (Recently) Immigrated and Refugee Teachers. https://blog.hf.uni-koeln.de/immigrated-and-refugee-teachers-requal/digital-library/.

Kelchtermans, G. (2009). Career stories as gateway to understanding teacher development. In Bayer, M., Brinkkjær, U., Plauborg, H. & Rolls, S. (eds.), *Teachers' Career Trajectories and Work Lives: Professional Learning and Development in Schools and Higher Education*. Dordrecht: Springer, pp. 29–47.

Korthagen, F. A. (2013). In search of the essence of a good teacher: Toward a more holistic approach in teacher education. *Teaching and Teacher Education*, 20(1), pp. 77–97. doi:10.1108/S1479-3687(2013)0000019015.

Kreber, C. (ed.). (2009). *The University and Its Disciplines: Teaching and Learning Within and Beyond Disciplinary Boundaries*. New York: Routledge.

Kwee, C. T. T. (2023). Chinese immigrant teachers' motivation for teaching heritage language in Australia: A qualitative study. *International Journal of Instruction*, 16(1), pp. 333–356. https://doi.org/10.29333/iji.2023.16119a.

Kwee, C. T. T. (2020). Self-efficacy of immigrant teachers in Australia: A literature review. *Universal Journal of Educational Research*, 8(10), pp. 4440–4448. https://doi.org/10.13189/ujer.2020.081011.

Käck, A. (2018). Review: Global perspectives on teaching excellence – A new era for higher education. *Högre utbildning*, 8(1), pp. 42–43. doi: 10.23865/hu.v8.1238.

Käck, A. (2019a). Digital Competence and Ways of Thinking and Practising in Swedish Teacher Education: Experiences by teachers with a foreign teaching degree. Diss. Stockholm University. http://urn.kb.se/resolve?urn=urn:nbn:se:su:diva-171460.

Käck, A. (2019b). The use of digital technologies in Swedish teacher education: Experiences by migrant teachers. In Daniela, L. (ed.), *Innovations, Technologies and Research in Education*, University of Latvia Press, pp. 129–151. https://doi.org/10.22364/atee.2019.itre.

Käck, A. (2020a). Migrant teachers in Swedish teacher education and their re-entry as professionals. In Kremsner, G. Proyer, M. & Biewer, G. (eds.), *Inklusion von Lehrkräften nach der Flucht: Über universitäre Ausbildung zum beruflichen Wiedereinstieg.* Bad Heilbrunn: Verlag Julius Klinkhardt.

Käck, A. (2020b) Swedish teacher education and migrant teachers. *Intercultural Education*, 31(2), pp. 260–264. https://doi.org/10.1080/14675986.2019.1702329.

Käck, A., Männikkö Barbutiu, S. & Fors, U. (2019b). Migrant teachers' self-estimated digital competence – a study within Swedish teacher education. *Contemporary Issues in Technology and Teacher Education*, 19(2), pp. 256–278. www.citejournal.org/volume-19/issue-2-19/general/migrant-teachers-self-estimated-digital-competence-a-study-within-swedish-teacher-education/.

Käck, A. & Männikkö Barbutiu, S. (2012). *Digital Competence in Teacher Education.* [Digital kompetens I lärarutbildningen]. Lund: Studentlitteratur.

Käck, A., Männikkö Barbutiu, S. & Fors, U. G. H. (2018a). Unfamiliar ways of thinking and practising in teacher education: Experiences by migrant teachers. In Sablić, M., Škugor, A. & Đurđević Babić, I. (eds.), *Proceedings of the 42nd ATEE Annual Conference 2017 in Dubrovnik, Croatia: Changing Perspectives and Approaches in Contemporary Teaching* (pp. 219–235). Brussels, Belgium: Association for Teacher Education in Europe.

Käck, A., Männikkö Barbutiu, S. & Fors, U. G. H. (2018b). Migrant teachers' experiences with the use of digital technology and media during their placement period in Swedish schools. In Heijnen, M. de Hei, M. & van Ginkel, S. (eds.), *Proceedings of the ATEE Winter Conference: Technology and Innovative Learning 2018* (pp. 63–71). Utrecht, Netherlands: Archimedes Institute, Utrecht University of Applied Sciences, and Association of Teacher Education in Europe

Käck, A., Roll-Pettersson, L., Alai-Rosales, S. S. et al. (2014). Intercultural blended design considerations: A case study of a Nordic-Baltic course in autism intervention. *European Journal of Open, Distance and E-Learning*, 17(1), pp. 93–107. https://doi.org/10.2478/eurodl-2014-0006.

Lawless, K. A. & Pellegrino, J. W. (2007). Professional development in integrating technology into teaching and learning: Knowns, unknowns, and ways to pursue better questions and answers. *Educational Research*, 77, pp. 575–614. https://doi.org/10.3102/0034654307309921.

Lee, S. & Schallert, D. L. (2016). Becoming a teacher: Coordinating past, present, and future selves with perspectival understandings about teaching. *Teaching and Teacher Education*, 56, pp. 72–83. https://doi.org/10.1016/j.tate.2016.02.004.

Lefever, S., Berman, R., Guojónsdóttir, H. & Gísaladóttir, K. R. (2014). Professional identities of teachers with an immigrant background. *Netla– Online Journal on Pedagogy and Education, Special Issue 2014 – Diversity in Education: Teachers and Learners*, pp.1–16.

Malm, S. (2019). Bridging programmes for migrant teachers and preschool teachers in Sweden. In Kremsner, G., Proyer, M. & Biewer, G. (eds.), *Inklusion von Lehrkräften nach der Flucht: Über universitäre Ausbildung zum beruflichen Wiedereinstieg*. Bad Heilbrunn: Verlag Julius Klinkhardt.

Malm, S. (2019). Personal communication May to June 2019 and 28 December 2022. The Office of Human Science, the Coordination Section for Commissioned Education.

Malm. S. & Åström, A. Personal communication, 4 June 2019. The Office of Human Science, the Coordination Section for Commissioned Education.

Masoumi, D. & Noroozi, O. (2023). Developing early career teachers' professional digital competence: a systematic literature review. *European Journal of Teacher Education*, 46(1), pp. 1–23. doi: 10.1080/02619768 .2023.2229006.

Marom, L. (2017). Mapping the field: Examining the recertification of internationally educated teachers. *Canadian Journal of Education / Revue canadienne de l'éducation*, 40(3), pp. 157–190.

Marom, L. (2019). From experienced teachers to newcomers to the profession: The capital conversion of internationally educated teachers in Canada. *Teaching and Teacher Education*, 78, pp. 85–96. https://doi.org/10.1016/j.tate .2018.11.006.

Mezirow, J. (1975). *Education for Perspective Transformation: Women's Reentry Programs in Community Colleges*. New York: Columbia University.

Mezirow, J. (1978a). Perspective Transformation. *Adult Education*, 28(2), pp. 100–110. https://doi.org/10.1177/074171367802800202.

Mezirow, J. & Marsick, V. (1978b). *Education for Perspective Transformation: Women's Re-entry Programs in Community College*. New York: Columbia University.

Mezirow, J. (1991). *Transformative Dimensions of Adult Learning*. San Francisco: Jossey-Bass.

McCune, V. & Hounsell, D. (2005). The development of students' ways of thinking and practising in three final-year biology courses. *Higher Education*, 49(3), pp. 255–289.

McCune, V. & Reimann, N. (2002). The Enhancing Teaching-Learning Environments in Undergraduate Courses Project: Some initial reflections and observations. Paper presented at the 10th Improving Student Learning Symposium, Brussels, September 2002.

Meyer, J. & Land, R. (2003). Threshold concepts and troublesome knowledge: Linkages to ways of thinking and practising within the disciplines. Occasional, Enhancing Teaching-Learning Environments in Undergraduate Course Project No. 4. University of Edinburgh.

Meyer, J. & Land, R. (2005). Threshold concepts and troublesome knowledge (2): Epistemological considerations and a conceptual framework for teaching and learning. *Higher Education*, 49(3), pp. 373–388. https://doi.org/10.1007/s10734-004-6779-5.

Meyer, J., Land, R. & Baillie, C. (eds.). (2010). *Threshold Concepts and Transformational Learning*. Rotterdam: Sense Publishers.

Mezirow, J. (1978). Perspective transformation. *Adult Education*, 28(2), pp. 100–110. https://doi.org/10.1177/074171367802800202.

Miller, P. W. (2018). Overseas trained teachers (OTTs) in England: Surviving or thriving? *Management in Education*, 32(4), pp. 160–166. https://doi.org/10.1177/0892020618795201.

Miller, P. (2019). Aspiration, career progression and overseas trained teachers in England. *International Journal of Leadership in Education*, 22(1), pp. 55–68.

Ministry of Education and Research. (1992). Högskolelagen 1992:1434. [Higher Education Act 1992:1434]. www.riksdagen.se/sv/dokument-lagar/dokument/svensk-for-[2018-05-31].

Ministry of Education and Research in Sweden. (2011). Högskoleförordningen 2011:326. [The Higher Education Ordinance 2011:326]. Ordinance on eligibility and certification for teachers and preschool teachers. www.riksdagen.se/sv/dokument-lagar/dokument/svensk-for-fattningssamling/forordning-2011326-om-behorighet-och_sfs-2011-326.

Ministry of Education and Research. (2014a). Högskoleförordningen 2014:1096, Kapitel 2. [The Higher Education Ordinance 2014:1096, Annex 2]. www.uhr.se/en/start/laws-and-regulations/Laws-and-regulations/The-Higher-Education-Ordinance/Annex-2/.

Ministry of Education and Research in Sweden. (2014b). Högskoleför- ordningen 2008:1101. [The Higher Education Ordinance 2018:1101]. Ordinance on Higher Education which supplements a completed foreign education. www.riks-dagen.se/sv/dokument-lagar/dokument/svensk-for-fattnings-samling/forordning-20081101-om-hogskoleutbildning-som_sfs-2008-1101.

Ministry of Education and Research. (2016). Law on recognition of professional qualifications. Sweden. www.riks-dagen.se/sv/dokument-lagar/dokument/svensk-forfattnings-samling/lag-2016145-om-erkannande-av_sfs-2016-145.

Moloney, R. & Saltmarsh, D. (2016). 'Knowing your students' in the culturally and linguistically diverse classroom. *Australian Journal of Teacher Education*, 41(4), pp. 79–93.

National Agency for Education. (2013). *Curriculum for the Upper Secondary School*. [Läroplan för gymnasieskolan: Lgy 11. Revised 2018]. Stockholm: Skolverket.

National Agency for Education. (2022). *Curriculum for the Compulsory School, Preschool Class and School-Age Educare*. [Läroplan för grundskolan, förskoleklassen och fritidshemmet, Lgr 11. Revised 2018.] Stockholm: Skolverket.

National Agency for Education. (2019). *Curriculum for the Preschool*. [Läroplan för förskolan: Lpfö 18]. Stockholm: Skolverket.

Nguyen, P.-M., Terlouw, C. & Pilot, A. (2006). Culturally appropriate pedagogy: The case of group learning in a Confucian heritage culture context. *Intercultural Education*, 17, pp. 1–19. https://doi.org/10.1080/14675980500 502172.

Norberg, K. (2000). Intercultural education and teacher education in Sweden. *Teaching and Teacher Education*, 4, p. 511.

Nordic Council of Ministers. (2017a). Utdanning, arbeid og integrering i Norden – Kartlegging av godkjenningsordninger for utenlandske utdanninger, yrkeskvalifikasjoner og kompletterende utdanninger. Delrapport 1, TemaNord 2017:556. http://dx.doi.org/10.6027/TN2017-556.

Nordic Council of Ministers. (2017b). Utdanning, arbeid og integrering i Norden – Kartlegging av godkjenningsordninger for utenlandske utdanninger, yrkeskvalifikasjoner og kompletterende utdanninger. Delrapport 2, TemaNord 2017:557. http://dx.doi.org/10.6027/TN2017-557.

Owens, R. A. (2018). Transition experiences of new rural nurse practitioners. *The Journal for Nurse Practitioners*, 14(8), pp. 605–612. https://doi.org/10.1016/j.nurpra.2018.05.009.

Peeler, E. & Jane, B. (2005). Mentoring: Immigrant teachers bridging professional practices. *Teaching Education*, 16(4), pp. 325–336.

Proyer, M., Pellech, C., Kremsner, G. et al. (2019). IO1–Transnational Framework. Comparative Analysis of the Administrative Frameworks on the (Re-)Qualification Situation of Internationally Trained Teachers in Austria, Germany and Sweden https://blog.hf.uni-koeln.de/immigrated-and-refugee-teachers-requal/.

Puranen, B. (2019). Med migranternas röst. Den subjektiva integrationen, Forskningsrapport, 2.

Redecker, C. (2017, November). European framework for the digital competence of educators: DigCompEdu (Report No. JRC107466). https://doi.org/10.2760/159770.

Rosenow-Gerhard, J. (2021). *Entrepreneurial Learning. Learning Processes Within a Social Innovation Lab Through the Lens of Illeris Learning Theory.*

Cham: Springer International Publishing. https://doi.org/10.1007/978-3-030-85060-9_8.

Ryan, J. & Carroll, J. (2005). Canaries in the coal mine: International students in Western universities. In Carroll, J. & Ryan, J. (eds.), *Teaching International Students: Improving Learning for All*. London: Routledge, pp. 3–10.

Sadaf, A. & Johnson, B. L. (2017). Teachers' beliefs about integrating digital literacy into classroom practice: An investigation based on the theory of planned behavior. *Journal of Digital Learning in Teacher Education*, 33(4), pp. 129–137. https://doi.org/10.1080/21532974.2017.1347534.

Schmidt, D. A., Baran, E. & Thompson, A. D. (2009). Technological Pedagogical Content Knowledge (TPACK): The development and validation of an assessment instrument for preservice teachers. *Journal of Research on Technology in Education*, 42(2), pp. 123–149. doi:10.1080/15391523.2009.10782544.

Schmidt, C. & Schneider, J. (eds.), (2016). *Diversifying the Teaching Force in Transnational Contexts: Critical Perspectives*. Cham, Switzerland: Springer.

Skantz-Åberg, E., Lantz-Andersson, A., Lundin, M., & Williams, P. (2022). Teachers' professional digital competence: an overview of conceptualisations in the literature. *Cogent Education*, 9(1), 2063224. doi:10.1080/2331186X.2022.2063224.

Sjögren, A. & Ramberg, I. (eds) (2005). *Kvalitet och mångfald i högskoleutbildning: erfarenheter från interkulturell lärarutbildning [Quality and diversity in higher education: experiences from intercultural teacher education]*. Tumba: Mångkulturellt centrum.

Stockholm University. (2017). Account for the year 2017. [Årsredovisning 2017. Dnr SU FV-1.1.8-3030-17]. www.su.se/medar-betare/ekonomi/%C3%A5rsredovisning/%C3%A5rsredovisningar-tidigare-%C3%A5r.

Stensmo, C. (1994). Pedagogik och teoretisk filosofi. *Pedagogisk filosofi*. [Teaching philosophy]. Lund: Studentlitteratur, pp. 25–36.

Stensmo, C. (2007). *Pedagogisk filosofi*. [Teaching philosophy]. Stockholm: Studentlitteratur.

Taylor, E. (2009). Fostering transformative learning. In Mezirow, J. & Taylor, E. (eds.), *Transformative Learning in Practice: Insights from Community, Workplace, and Higher Education*. San Francisco, CA: Jossey-Bass.

Taylor, E. W. & Cranton, P. (2012). *Handbook of Transformative Learning: Theory, Research, and Practice*. San Francisco, CA: Jossey-Bass. https://ebookcen-tral-proquest-com.ezp.sub.su.se.

Terhart, H., Frantik, P., Bakkar, A. et al. (2020). IO3 – Method Toolbox "Heterogeneity in Schools and Higher Education in Europe": Teaching and Learning Methods for Programmes for (Recently) Immigrated and Refugee

Teachers in Higher Education. https://blog.hf.uni-koeln.de/immigrated-and-refugee-teachers-requal/toolbox-2/.

Thomas, E. (1997). Developing a culture-sensitive pedagogy: Tackling a problem of melding 'global culture' within existing cultural contexts. *International Journal of Educational Development*, 17, pp. 13–26. https://doi.org/10.1016/S0738-0593(96)00066-1.

Vandeyar, S., Vandeyar, T., & Elufisan, K. (2014). Impediments to the successful reconstruction of African immigrant teachers' professional identities in South African schools. *South African Journal of Education*, 34(2), pp. 1–20.

Venkatesh, V., Brown, S. A., & Bala, H. (2013). Bridging the qualitative-quantitative divide: Guidelines for conducting mixed methods research in information systems. *MIS Quarterly*, 37(1), pp. 21–54. doi:10.25300/MISQ/2013/37.1.02.

Walsh, S. C., Brigham, S. M., & Wang, Y. (2011). Internationally educated female teachers in the neoliberal context: Their labour market and teacher certification experiences in Canada. *Teaching and Teacher Education*, 27(3), pp. 657–665. https://doi.org/10.1016/j.tate.2010.11.004.

Wen, B., Wang, Q., Gooden, A. et al. (2023). The Dual-Challenge of Teaching Online in a Foreign Land: Understanding Western Foreign Teachers' Professional Identity and Confidence Development via a Transformative Learning Lens. *Asia-pacific Education Researcher* [Preprint]. https://doi.org/10.1007/s40299-023-00723-3.

Yan, D. (2021). The impact of mentoring on a non-native immigrant teacher's professional development. *Teaching and Teacher Education*, 103, 103348. https://doi.org/10.1016/j.tate.2021.103348.

Yip, S. Y. (2023). Immigrant teachers' experience of professional vulnerability. *Asia-Pacific Journal of Teacher Education*, 51(3), pp. 233–247. https://doi.org/10.1080/1359866X.2023.2174075.

Yip, S. Y., Saito, E., & Diamond, Z. M. (2022). Professional identity and agency in immigrant teachers' professional transition to work in Australia. *The Australian Educational Researcher*, 51(1), pp. 1–18. https://doi.org/10.1007/s13384-022-00600-w.

Zhao, Y., & Ko, J., (2018). Workplace learning in the professional development of vocational education teachers. *Studia Paedagogica*, 23(2), pp. 43–58.

Cambridge Elements ≡

Critical Issues in Teacher Education

Tony Loughland
University of New South Wales

Tony Loughland is an Associate Professor in the School of Education at the University of New South Wales, Australia. Tony is currently leading projects on using AI for citizens' informed participation in urban development, the provision of staffing for rural and remote areas in NSW and on Graduate Ready Schools.

Andy Gao
University of New South Wales

Andy Gao is a Professor in the School of Education at the University of New South Wales, Australia. He edits various internationally-renowned journals, such as International Review of Applied Linguistics in Language Teaching for De Gruyter and Asia Pacific Education Researcher for Springer.

Hoa T. M. Nguyen
University of New South Wales

Hoa T. M. Nguyen is an Associate Professor in the School of Education at the University of New South Wales, Australia. She specializes in teacher education/development, mentoring and sociocultural theory.

About the Series
This series addresses the critical issues teacher educators and teachers are engaged with in the increasingly complex profession of teaching. These issues reside in teachers' response to broader social, cultural and political shifts and the need for teachers' professional education to equip them to teach culturally and linguistically diverse students.

Cambridge Elements ☰

Critical Issues in Teacher Education

Elements in the Series

Interculturality, Criticality and Reflexivity in Teacher Education
Fred Dervin

Enhancing Educators' Theoretical and Practical Understandings of Critical Literacy
Vera Sotirovska and Margaret Vaughn

Reclaiming the Cultural Politics of Teaching and Learning: Schooled in Punk
Greg Vass

Language Teacher's Social Cognition
Hao Xu

Who am I as a Teacher? Migrant Teachers' Redefined Professional Identity
Annika Käck

A full series listing is available at: www.cambridge.org/EITE

Printed in the United States
by Baker & Taylor Publisher Services